From Citizen to Refugee

Uganda Asians come to Britain

From Citizen to Refugee

Uganda Asians come to Britain

Mahmood Mamdani

THIRD EDITION

with a new introduction by the author

Daraja Press

Published by
Daraja Press
https://darajapress.com

From Citizen to Refugee:
Uganda Asians Come To Britain, 3rd edition
With a new Introduction by Mahmood Mamdani

First edition published by Frances Pinter 1973
Second edition published by Pambazuka Press 2011

Cover design: Kate McDonnell
Cover photo © PA/PA Archive/Press Association Images

Library and Archives Canada Cataloguing in Publication

Title: From citizen to refugee : Uganda Asians come to Britain / Mahmood
    Mamdani.
Names: Mamdani, Mahmood, 1946- author.
Description: Third edition.
Identifiers: Canadiana 20220278652 | ISBN 9781990263514 (softcover)
Subjects: LCSH: Mamdani, Mahmood, 1946- | LCSH: South Asians–
    Uganda–Social conditions. | LCSH: South Asians–Great Britain–Social
    conditions. | LCSH: Refugees–Uganda–Social conditions. | LCSH:
    Refugees–Great Britain–Social conditions. | LCGFT: Autobiographies.
Classification: LCC DT433.242 .M36 2022 | DDC 325/.210967610941–
    dc23

PART ONE

PART TWO

What Have We Learnt Over a Half Century?

Mahmood Mamdani

Mahmood Mamdani is Herbert Lehman Professor of Government at Columbia University and was director and Professor at Makerere Institute of Social Research (2010-2022).

text based on an address at the 50th anniversary commemoration of the expulsion of Asians from Uganda in 1972, Refugee Law Society, Makerere University, August 19, 2022

I left Uganda in November 1972, during the last week of the expulsion, for a refugee camp in London. Six months later, I took my first academic job at the University of Dar es Salaam. After the fall of Amin, I came to Kampala as a frontier intern-in-mission with the All-Africa Conference of Churches, with an office at the Church of Uganda headquarters in Mengo. The next year, 1980, I joined Makerere University. I made a point to ask most people I met about their thoughts on the expulsion; almost all responded that it was bad how Amin did it. I realized that most Ugandans did not oppose the expulsion. This was the beginning of wisdom for me.

Ten years later, I began asking the same question to friends, neighbors and school mates from pre-'72 Uganda days, wherever I met them, in Kampala or Britain. To my surprise, over 90% said they would not want to return to pre-'72 days in Uganda. They too were not opposed to the expulsion.

My first observation: how come over 90% of residents of the country, brown or black, would not want to return to the days and years before the 1972 expulsion?

The expulsion cannot just be understood as an event that occurred in 1972. The event needs to be understood as a culmination of a process. Long before 1972, many Ugandan Asians had been disenfranchised by law, both Ugandan and British.

The 'independence' Constitution of 1962 had a citizenship clause. Citizenship by birth is restricted to those who were born to Ugandan parents and one of whose grandparents was also born in Uganda.

My guess is that no more than 10% of people of Asian descent with permanent residence in Uganda would have qualified for citizenship under this clause.

The 1995 Constitution changed the substituted individual requirements for citizenship by birth to a 'group' requirement. The group had to be indigenous to the country. Schedule 3 of the 1995 Constitution had a list of 'indigenous' tribes. By this criterion, no Uganda Asian could be a citizen by birth after 1995.

Under British law, Asian residents of Uganda lost the right of entry (or return) to the U.K. after 1968 even if they were holders of British passports.

My second observation: We need to distinguish between two different groups of Asians, those pre-'72 and those post-'85. For the first group, Uganda was home. For most of the second, Uganda is a temporary abode, a point of transit. I will focus on the first group.

What have we learnt over a half century?

Learning is both an individual and a collective experience. One way to answer the question is to identify new knowledge on the expulsion, produced over the past fifty years. I focus here on four books:

The first is Ian Sanjay Patel's study of British immigration policy, titled *We're Here Because You Were There: Immigration and the End of Empire*, published in 2021.

Sanjay Patel's book begins with the 1968 act which differentiated between two groups of British citizens: white and non-white; historical and non-historical; distinguishing kith and kin from others. During the Asian expulsion, the British cabinet and bureaucracy came up with a new language to make this same racialized distinction: white 'belongers' vs non-white UKPH (United Kingdom Passport Holders).

The effect of these two sets of legislations, in Uganda and Britain, was like that of a pincer movement that disenfranchised many before any were expelled. These many ran into tens of thousands.

Uganda Asians as Victims

There has developed, since 1972, a global industry portraying Uganda Asians as victims. Few in my generation, the first generation of those expelled, wrote of our experience. As a people, we were not chroniclers. We were also not given to reflecting on our own experiences critically. It is the children of refugees – second generation – who have attempted to address this deficit. These hand-me-down stories have gradually homogenized into victim narratives.

Uganda Asians are a poor fit as victims.

For a start, the expulsion meant different things for different groups of Uganda Asians. For a substantial group, the lowest estimates are upwards of twelve thousand, the expulsion liberated them from an impossible situation.

According to intelligence reports, anywhere upwards of ten thousand Asian residents of Uganda were stateless by 1971. They were without a right to work in the country. At first, they lived in places of worship – temples, mosques, gurudwaras. With an increase in numbers, they overflowed into one-room tenements; in the words of Bob Astles, intelligence officer under both Obote and Amin, these resembled 'concentration camp like conditions.'

This group celebrated the expulsion. At the other extreme were the group of industrialists and merchants, maybe a few thousand if you include family members.

One book stands out in the chorus that I call the Expulsion Industry for its rare honesty. This is Neema Shah's portrayal of an Indian family in her recent novel, *Kololo Hill: A Novel*, Picador, New Delhi, 2021. The novel is written through the eyes of Asha, the newly married Jinja-based daughter-in-law of a wealthy merchant family living on Kololo Hill. It narrates her journey of discovery, day by day, of lies and deceptions common to her shopkeeper husband Pran, forcing her eyes to open to an entire culture of lies and deceptions that had become so much a part of life for Indian business families that they seemed normal and no longer abhorrent. As her world unravels, it peels like an onion, layer by layer, bringing the daily business of the Asian merchant community to light and raises a big question mark about the now standard and uniform story of the Asian victims of theft, rape, violence, now commonplace in the genre of expulsion stories.

It is worth noting that there was no large-scale loss of life during the expulsion. In a land known for sporadic massacres, there were no massacres of Asians. When massacres happened, they were of 'indigenous' people. Also, there was hardly any large-scale theft. This should not be surprising. Given that the expulsion itself was one big generalized theft, it left little room for individual thefts. Amin's soldiers were on the alert: their orders were to make sure that no ordinary soldier tamper with property that was to pass on to one officer or another. The thefts that took place were few and far between.

One common loss united those expelled in 1972. This was the loss of home. A sense of belonging develops over generations. The generation that was expelled lived as 'strangers', *musafir* in Hindustani. Where ever they landed, they lived as if always ready to pack their bags and leave at short notice. Many of their houses had more the feel of guest houses rather than homes.

Amin as a Master Perpetrator

The flip side of Asian victim narratives has been another industry, equally a chorus, united by a single aim, to demonize Amin as an uncivilized brute. Mark Leopold's 2020 book, *Idi Amin*, shines a critical light on the barrage of writings and media depictions of Amin that followed three expulsions, first of the Israelis, then of Uganda Asians, and then of the British. This book is not on Amin, nor on his self-proclaimed victims, but on how the discourse on Amin changed direction from praising Amin, as a noble savage who delivered the country and the continent from the erratic dictatorship of Obote to demonizing the same Amin as an African Pol Pot (in the words of a British minister who had earlier ordered Amin's assassination). Leopold's point is that these books would be better read as a source of knowledge on those who wrote them than on Amin, who they purported to write about.

Lwanga-Lunyiigo's Redefinition of Uganda as an Indian Colony

The last book that merits inclusion in this slim reading list is Lwanga Lunyiigo's *Uganda, an Indian Colony*. Lunyiigo is a Makerere historian who had previously written two great books, one on Muwanga, the kabaka who fought the British at the turn of twentieth century, and the other on the land question. He is also a good friend. The title is a stunner. It provokes, almost compelling the passerby to buy it. The title is a publisher's dream. Most of us are used to thinking of Uganda as a British colony. But an Indian colony? Is this a commercial ploy, I asked myself. But then, almost habitually, I turned to the back side of the jacket which reads: "The long and short of this book is that it puts the spotlight on Indians in East Africa narrating them as deputy imperialists, sub-imperialist, privileged workers of the colonialists." Between the front cover and the back of the jacket, two things change: one, Professor Lunyiigo's claim broadens, he now passes a verdict on not just Ugandan Indians, but Indians in all of East Africa; second, his claim is less ambitious, Indians are no longer said to be a colonial power onto themselves, they are now "privileged workers" of these colonialists. According to this back side of the jacket, the Bayindi were really sub-imperialists.

Sub-imperialism or Indirect Rule?

There has been a whole tradition of Ugandan history writing that talks of Buganda as a sub-imperial power, one that was vital to the conquest of most of Uganda. The story begins with the conquest of the Kingdom of Bunyoro-Kitara, then of the rest of the country. The claim triggered a widespread debate in the 1960s and 70s: Was Buganda an imperial power, even if a subordinate one? Or was Baganda itself colonized, even if a large section of the elite was in service of Britain, the imperial power? In short, were the Baganda part of the enemy or part of the oppressed people of Uganda, even if complicit in the oppression?

The debate only changed with the change of paradigm, from 'sub-imperialism' to 'indirect rule'. The debate changed when we recognized that the very nature of colonialism had changed, from "direct rule" whereby imperial powers took direct charge of conquest and administration to "indirect rule" whereby colonial powers looked to harness junior partners, allies, whether local or not-so-local, native or immigrant, to do the dirty work of conquest and daily administration. In return they got privileges, sometimes square miles of land, but they remained colonized. The notion of indirect rule put paid to the sub-imperial paradigm. *Why, one wonders, has Professor Lunyiigo resurrected this paradigm, going so far as to remove the qualifying adjective "sub-imperial" in his title?*

The two paradigms – 'sub-imperialism' and 'indirect rule' – have opposite political implications. Sub-imperial agents are considered part of the enemy; agents of indirect rule are considered potential allies, with a place in the anti-colonial united front. In the 1960s, the theorists of Buganda sub-imperialism held up Buganda as the last relic of British colonialism, part of the enemy of the Ugandan people. For Professor Lunyiigo, it is Indians, whether colonisers or sub-imperial agents, who are part of the enemy. Why, one wonders, has Lwanga-Lunyiigo resurrected this paradigm, even going so far as to remove the qualifying adjective "sub-imperial" in his title?

Good historians have the skill to dig into archives and come up with little-known or even previously hidden facts. Lwanga-Lunyiigo is a historian. There are some facts in this book that I would dispute. There is no evidence to show that Indians who made it good in post-'72 Britain had brought their seed capital from Uganda. Even if we grant that most facts marshalled by Professor Lunyiigo are verifiable we need to acknowledge that facts do not make an argument. It is the argument that provides the framework into which to arrange facts. The riddle of Lwanga-Lunyiigo's book is that he announces the framework in the title, dilutes it in the back of the jacket, and abandons it in the bulk of the book. If the title sums up the argument, then the argument never appears in the rest of the book.

For Uganda Asians, however, it is important to read this book for it is sure to provide an important source of self-critique. When I read Lunyiigo's account of the conferences Amin had held with Uganda Asian leaders in the months before the expulsion, I was outraged at the historical failure of these so-called leaders. Amin opened the first conference with a list of Indian shortcomings – social exclusion; a business culture rife with deception and lies; a self-justifying racism that rationalized petty privileges colonialism conferred on them while at the same time blaming the British for the colonial legacy; and a weak commitment to either the larger society or the country at large. He then went on to invite the same leaders to reflect as a community on the way forward, which these so-called leaders refused to do – because, they said, we are a small group who can only leave it to the government to define the way forward. At what was a critical juncture in the history of both the country and the Asian minority, this was akin to abdicating responsibility.

But this response also illuminates their larger character. The Asian leaders were an economic elite, not a political elite. They never aspired to power, unlike other minorities in the region, say white settlers, the Nubi or the Tutsi. Their political instinct was never to usurp power but always to nestle close to those in power, to look up to them for a road map to a future. They aimed to control the market, not the state. Minorities who aspired to rule, like the Tutsi or the Nubi or white settlers, were at times the target of genocidal projects. But not the Asians; they would be expelled, but not killed.

Asians in Uganda, as in East or Southern Africa, were immigrants, not settlers. The difference is telling: immigrants are prepared to be a part of the political community to which they move; settlers aim to create their own political community, a colony, more precisely, settler colonialism. Settlers are always at odds with the native communities among whom they live. It is difficult to find a settler without a gun. It is just as difficult to think of a dukawalla with a gun. As an individual, the Indian dukawalla is proverbially known for accommodation, even timidity. This is hardly the human materials from which to make conquerors or colonists. It is, though, the material from which to craft merchants. When an elite emerged from communities of dukawallas, they were an economic elite, not a political elite. [When Indians used guns during the 1958 trade boycott, these were the plantation owners, not the dukawallas, both Indians, but members of different classes.]

The political elite is more likely to strategize the future; the economic elite is more likely to accommodate to it. Even when champions of industry or trade, like the Madhvanis under Obote 1, aim at 'state capture', they do so in collaboration with existing political leaders. They do not become political leaders; they aim, at most, to nestle with ministers, even presidents.

There are, of course, exceptions, such as Rajat Neogy, the editor of *Transition* in Uganda at the dawn of independence, or Pio Gama Pinto and Makhan Singh and others in Kenya. But they were not "Asian" political leaders, neither in their calling, nor their imagination nor the following they mobilized. May be this is why they do not find a place in Lwanga-Lunyiigo's narrative. For they do not fit his argument.

But as we think of the Asian legacy fifty years after, I leave you with five observations:

1. There is no one Asian legacy. There are several, and they are contradictory. Not all are legacies we would like to wipe out from our collective memories. Some we would like to build on; others we would like to reform.

2. The Asian question can allow us to think the larger Ugandan question. Think of any of the big questions in this country: the Baganda question, the Northern question, the Karamoja question and the Asian question. There is one thing common among these four: the state has

always claimed the right to solve each of these on behalf of society, and always through violence. And it has never succeeded. The result has always been perverse. State strategy has always been to set up one group or another – the Baganda at one point, the Asians at another, the northerners after 1986, and the Karimojong all through our post-independence history – as the enemy of society.

3. The great strength of African societies in the pre-colonial period had been the ability to absorb newcomers, immigrants. The Baganda, for example, are said to have begun as four clans in the 13th century; over centuries, they have absorbed both immigrants and 'indigenous' or 'originals' and those not. The African tradition is to integrate, not to segregate. Look around the continent. The capacity to integrate has been common to the Amhara, the Arabs, the Hausa, the Waswahili, the Zulu and others.

The newly independent East African countries followed the colonial tradition, and not the tradition of pre-colonial societies. The clause on 'citizenship' in the independence constitution of Uganda distinguished 'indigenous' from 'non-indigenous' residents, not those born in Uganda from those not, not between residents and non-residents. Indigeneity was defined by having at least one grandparent born in Uganda. This ruled out at least 90% of Asian residents of Uganda from a birthright to citizenship.

The 1995 Constitution further entrenched this prejudice by acknowledging 'indigenous' groups (tribes) in law. After 1995, this government restructured local government by multiplying district boundaries on the principle that each minority be recognized as 'indigenous' and granted its own district. The alternative would be to acknowledge the equality of all residents in a territory.

4. The Asian question has not gone away; it remains. But it is no longer the original Asian question. The new Asian question emerged in the Museveni period. It has two features: One, the new Asians are not considered Ugandans even if some of them may hold Uganda passports. For President Museveni, they are "investors", not citizens. As investors, they are bearers of property, not of rights. They have neither political rights, nor political obligations. They may be here year after year, but they live as permanent strangers, without obligation to community or

country. In the African imagination, they have become the prototype of a mercenary community. For the Asians, they live on sufferance, always on guard, never at peace. We may ask ourselves: in whose interest is this state of affairs? Surely, not in the interest of those identified as "Asians" nor of the people of this country. The question merits further reflection.

5. In the transition between two constitutions, 1972 and 1995, Ugandans have changed our notion of belonging. The 1995 Constitution defines entire groups, and not individuals, as "indigenous". Between constitutions, new groups try to petition parliament to be included in the list of "indigenous" groups. Several years ago, many such groups sent in petitions, including the Banyaruanda, the Somali, the Bayindi. President Museveni's response was to remind the Bayindi that the world is divided into continents. God made each continent for a different race: Europe is for whites, Asia for browns and yellows, and Africa for blacks. Like the notion of indigenous, this story lacks a sense of history, or its sense of history is based on biology. It has forgotten a basic historical fact: there is only one race, the human race, which began in Africa. It has also lost a sense of how the world is changing, including decolonization. Today, American law recognizes African Americans as Americans of African descent. One of the contenders for the post of prime minister in the U.K. this year (2022) was born in England of parents born in Kenya and Tanganyika respectively. The Indian and Pakistani states acknowledge the existence of South Asians of African origin, known as *Sidis*. There is a Sidi member of parliament in Pakistan. Some time ago, Ugandans of South Asian origin formed an organization, called the Asian African Association of Uganda. I leave you with words from their founding document:

> *Whether citizen or not, whether in the country for generations or fresh off the plane, all persons of South Asian descent in Uganda are identified as Bayindi. ... For someone who thinks of Uganda and Africa as home, to be called a Muyindi is to live in the past, to ignore our present, and to be blind to the future. It is to live in this land as if one were a visitor. You cannot be a permanent visitor: that is a ticket to permanent insecurity and permanent irresponsibility. This mindset is at the source of our continuing social*

and political isolation. ... We need to give a deep thought to who we really are, and what is our relationship to Africa and African society. We are not South Asians (Indians, Pakistani or Bangladeshi), for South Asians live in South Asia and are committed to making a future there. Nor are we overseas South Asians, who are part of a South Asian Diaspora whose members aim to return home to South Asia after a temporary sojourn overseas. True, our origin is South Asia, but our present is African. Many of us hope to make a future in Africa. We are Africans of Asian Origin, Asian Africans.

Preface to the Second Edition (2011)

I WROTE THIS BOOK in 1973 in a refugee transit camp on Kensington Church Street in London. The opportunity to write came as an act of necessity. One day, I received a telegram from Yash Tandon inviting me to have lunch with him at the London School of Economics. Professor Tandon, as I then called him, had been professor of political science at Makerere University in Kampala and had come to the London School of Economics as a visiting professor for a year. Little did he know that this would be the year of expulsion.

I telephoned Professor Tandon and told him that I could not afford the tube fare from Kensington to LSE but would be pleased to take up his offer if he would send me the fare by post. He did.

Yash had invited a former doctoral student of his to lunch. I talked of Kampala during the expulsion and the camp after, pouring my mind out, as we had lunch and then retired to Yash's office for tea. On the way out, Yash's former student, Frances Pinter, asked me if I would come to her house for dinner. I said the same terms applied: if she gave me the tube fare, I would happily come. She obliged and I turned up at her place a few days later.

Frances told me that she had finished her doctorate at LSE the previous year and had looked for jobs with publishers. However, she was only offered secretarial positions, so she had finally decided to become a publisher herself. If I would write of my experiences in Kampala before the expulsion and at the Kensington Camp afterwards, she would publish it as a book. I said I would if she gave me an advance of £200, the sum I needed to pay six months' rent in advance for a flat for my parents while I took up an offer to teach at the University of Dar es Salaam. She said she would give me the advance if I promised to write the book in three weeks, for her sense was that the appetite for a book on the Asian expulsion would be as short-lived as its public memory, which she counted in months, not years. I agreed.

Frances gave me a tape recorder into which to talk. She said she would transcribe my ruminations, as it would be quicker than my trying to write a draft. After a few days of trying to talk to the machine, I told Frances that I understood that she thought I came from an oral tradition and that I would find it easier to talk than to write, but the idea was simply not workable in practice. I asked for pen and paper, which she then provided.

I wrote the first draft in 20 days. Frances published it immediately. There was no edit and certainly no rewrite. With its publication, Frances became a publisher, Frances Pinter Ltd, and I began to think that I was indeed capable of writing more than one book. (I had written my first book, *The Myth of Population Control,* the year before as a graduate student at Harvard.) A decade and a half later, an Indian filmmaker called Mira Nair read the book and wrote to me that she intended to visit Uganda to research her new film, which she intended to base on the Asian expulsion. That research brought Mira and me together in lifelong partnership. I told Mira that she was my real royalty for writing the book.

I have taken advantage of this new edition – or, rather, I should say my editor, Shereen Karmali, has taken advantage of it – to correct typos in the original edition. But I have resisted the temptation to make any substantive changes, even where I find the original text wanting.

I should like to say a few words about the biggest change – or rather addition – I would make were I to get the opportunity to write about the Asian expulsion yet again. My present vantage point has been shaped by the long intellectual struggle that led to the publication of *Citizen and Subject* in 1996. From today's vantage point, then, the interpretation of events that drives the narrative in the current text is too narrow. It is encapsulated within the logic of the market but excludes the broad logic of the political.

The Asian expulsion was not simply a product of failed post-independence attempts to reform racially stratified market relations that had been forged under British colonial rule. It was, even more, a product of a failure to reform colonial statecraft. Had I made this connection then, I would have placed the expulsion in a broader history of modes of rule and not just relations in the marketplace. Colonial rule stabilised when it was successful in administrating the colonised as so many groups, each identified as a race or a tribe. When the groups concerned began to self-identify themselves as such in their relationship to the state, and eventually to one another, they became racialised and tribalised in their consciousness and organisation. (I think the term 'tribe' is better than the currently fashionable 'ethnic group' because it brings out more clearly the politi-co-administrative logic behind colonial statecraft.)

From the standpoint of the political, the Asian expulsion belongs to a larger history of ethnic cleansing. It may be said that colonialism began with an act of ethnic cleansing: using violence and law to put each 'tribe' and 'race' in its proper place. The history of establishment of British rule in Uganda is one of a series of acts of ethnic cleansing: forcibly removing Catholics (and Muslims) from Mengo (the capital of Buganda kingdom, adjacent to the new colonial capital, Kampala) to Masaka; then forcibly appropriating land from its users, the *bakopi* (peasants), to distribute it as so many colonial grants to members of the Baganda elite who had converted to Protestant Christianity and allied with the British, alongside a few Catholics and Muslims that the British judged politically 'moderate'; and, finally, dividing the whole of Buganda into so many denominational districts – 'Protestant', 'Catholic' and 'Muslim' – so that the entire population moved along with 'their' chiefs to 'their' newly designated denominational district.

The use of violence to target racialised or tribalised groups and thereby settle seemingly intractable social questions has been common to colonial rule. That practice has also been reproduced by post-colonial regimes. The Buganda crisis of 1966–67 – which I do not discuss – was its first stark manifestation. The expulsion of Kenyan workers in 1970 – which I do discuss – was the second. My point is that, bathed in a different hue, the logic and practices of colonial and post-colonial statecraft, the Asian expulsion would not only have been better illuminated but would also in turn have further illuminated the larger course of Uganda's history.

Having 'resettled' my parents in a rented London flat, I moved to take up my first academic job offer at the University of Dar es Salaam. That offer had been facilitated by the new dean of social sciences at the university, Professor Justinian Rweyemamu. I met Justinian when I joined Harvard in 1969. We were two of four students who formed a weekly study group with a radical faculty member in the Department of Economics, Arthur MacEwan. It is in this study group, for which we all received academic credit, that Justinian wrote the first draft of his PhD thesis, which would later be published as *Underdevelopment and Industrialisation in Tanzania*, and I wrote the first draft of my PhD thesis, later published as *Politics and Class Formation in Uganda*.

When today I think of my years at Harvard, I do not think of these as a time of great intellectual learning, but as a time of learning how to organise and act around major social issues. I spent more time in political meetings and demonstrations than I did in the classroom and library at Harvard. My deep involvement in the civil rights movement ('race'), the movement against the war in Vietnam ('anti-war') and the trade union movement ('class') was the heart of my Harvard experience. The University of Dar es Salaam, in contrast, was more of an intellectual experience. It started with Sunday morning 'ideological classes', organised at the same time as Sunday church service, as a deliberate secular affront to those with strong religious sentiments (I now think of it as an unwise and juvenile gesture).

And then it grew into study groups. At one time, in 1975, I remember having eight two-hour study groups in a week: one on Marx's *Capital*, another of the history of the three internationals, a third on the agrarian question, a fourth on the Chinese revolution, a fifth on the Russian revolution and so on. The irony is that, while we talked and discussed social change incessantly, we were hardly involved in any of the struggles (such as worker struggles that followed party guidelines, known as Mwongozo, to curb the arrogance of state functionaries in parastatals) that we wrote about. In my first years in Dar, I remember acutely missing my political and social involvement at Harvard.

The study group years at Dar ended with the beginning of what has come to be called 'the Dar debate'. The study groups closed, one after another, as their members took different sides in a debate which became increasingly sectarian and hostile. Erstwhile friends and comrades found it difficult to talk to one another as if to discuss with those with whom you disagreed was to revoke principle and betray a cause, as if the future of the world depended on this militant closed-mindedness. I now think of this as a mark of left intellectuals who were wont to substitute ourselves for social movements.

One of the groups that continued after the onset of the Dar debate was the Chang'ombe group, a study circle of Ugandans, both academics and those in town, actively committed to the anti-Amin struggle. When I returned to Kampala in 1979, it was as part of this group, and not as a returning 'Asian'.

I had neither family nor friends in Kampala. I stayed at the Imperial Hotel, in one of five rooms given to Yoweri Museveni, who had participated in the Chang'ombe group whenever he visited Dar from Moshi (in northern Tanzania). Museveni had given one of the rooms to his old comrade-in-arms, Augustine Ruzindana, a close friend and comrade of mine, who agreed to let me share the one bed in the room.

Return to Kampala was a difficult experience for me, full of mixed emotions. On the one hand, I was back in the city of my childhood and youth, one where I had gone to primary and secondary schools, where I knew literally every street – especially the Nakulabye–Bakuli–Mengo triangle in which we had lived for years – as though they were the lines on the palm of my hand. On the other hand, except for a few people, I did not know anyone in this city. How could this be? I remember walking the streets of Kampala day after day, week after week, and month after month, thinking of this question. All thoughts led to a single answer: the deeply racialised character of the urban society in which I had grown up, and of the institutional life that had shaped my outlook.

The Imperial Hotel then was a hotel full of returnees from exile. When night fell, everyone would go visiting relatives or friends who had never left. It was a great homecoming for all – except for me. There was one other person who shared this predicament, who was also friendless and familyless in this city. That was Laurent Kabila, who was to become Congo's first president in the post-Mobutu era. Kabila and I would sit together, evening after evening, in the foyer of the Imperial, and talk 'revolution' while everyone else went visiting and partying.

My only refuge then was the university. It was at Makerere, which I joined in 1980, that I found companionship and friendship. Those years at Makerere were for me a second growing up, a second coming of age, in Kampala. The Kampala I had grown up in as a child and a youth was deeply racialised; that Kampala was no more when I returned to the city in 1979. Bizarre as it may sound, even though I knew every street in this city, learning to live in this non-racial city was a wholly new experience.

I soon realised that, having no more than a dim memory of *bayindi* (Asians), most young people referred to me as *muzungu* (a white person). My only friends who could be called 'African' (as was the designation then and now of 'indigenous' Ugandans) were those with whom I had come from Dar es Salaam and others I had met through them. One of these was George Sekasi, chief engineer of the Railways. One evening, George and I were driving in his Railways Land Rover to his house, which was a few miles outside town on Gayaza Road. On the way, we were stopped by four or five Tanzanian soldiers who wanted a ride. Seated in the back seat, they talked in Kiswahili: 'This fellow is surely a Libyan. We should take him in the bush with us and finish him.'

George was quiet. I knew if I did not speak while we were still moving, this might be my last day on earth. '*Mimi ni Muganda,*' ('I am a Ugandan'), I began feebly.

They laughed. '*Muganda mweupe?*' ('A white Ugandan?') '*Mimi ni Muhindi. Nilikuwa mwalimu Chuo Kiku cha Dar-es-Salaam wakati wa Amin,*' I tried. ('I am an Indian. I was a professor at the University of Dar es Salaam during the Amin period.') They were quiet, not quite believing me, I thought. I persisted: '*Labda ninyi mesoma Azimio la* Arusha. *Inasema, mwanzoni, "Binadamu wote ni sawa".*' ('You have read the Arusha Declaration. It says at the very beginning, "All people are the same".')

After what seemed like a long silence, one said to his mates: '*Mwache. Huyu ni mwanasiasa.*' ('Leave him. He is political.')

When they left, I heaved a sigh of relief. But I would not forget the lesson I had learnt that day: even though I had come home, in the eyes of those who did not know me, I would be a foreigner. I knew I would never be able to take 'home' for granted.

Today's Kampala is more of a halfway house. The decisive break was President Museveni's decision to return expropriated properties to their former Asian owners. That single act brought back to Uganda members of the former Asian propertied class. Their numbers were insignificant, even today at most in the hundreds, but their impact was indeed significant. In their footsteps followed a new Asian immigration – from India, Pakistan and Bangladesh – of those who had never before been in Uganda, but who looked at it as a possible transition to greener pastures in the West.

The numbers of (South) Asians in Uganda at the time of writing – April 2011 – is roughly the same as that of Chinese and Europeans, between 30 and 40,000 in each case. The Europeans are mainly those in embassies and international NGOs, and professionals in South African firms. Most are transient. The Chinese range from peddlers on streets to shopkeepers and wholesalers, to construction workers. The (South) Asians, too, range from artisanal and commercial workers to professionals. What distinguishes this group is the presence of a small group of prominent capitalists. It is this group that defines the New Asian Question in today's Uganda, leading many an outsider to think that it is a simple continuation of the Old Asian Question.

My first encounter with popular perceptions of the New Indian Question came in 2004 when I took a sabbatical from Columbia University and came to Makerere. I brought my son along and put him in the Aga Khan primary, a local school where up to 5 per cent of the student body were of South Asian origin. One day, I went to see the teacher about how Zohran was doing. 'He is doing well,' said Mr Mwesigye, 'except that sometimes I do not always understand him.' I asked him to elaborate, and he told me the following story. One day, Mr Mwesigye asked in class that all Indian students raise their hand, since the headmaster had asked for a count of Indian students in each class. When the hands went up, he saw that Zohran had not raised his. When questioned, Zohran responded: 'I am not Indian, I am Ugandan!' The revelation to me was that Mr Mwesigye found this unusual.

The book you are about to read is about the Old Asian Question, about Asians who were the product of deeply racialised colonial institutions and yet saw Uganda as home. The New Asian Question, in contrast, is about those who live in racially mixed communities, whose children go to racially mixed schools and play in racially mixed grounds or parks or clubs, all of them defined by class more than race. Yet, these first generation immigrants are unlikely to see Uganda as home. They are likely to celebrate India's independence day with greater enthusiasm than the day of Uganda's independence.

If the Old Asian Question predates the Amin expulsion of 1972, the New Asian Question post-dates Museveni's return of properties in 1989. Its study must necessarily await an author with a deeper understanding of it than I can claim to possess.

INTRODUCTION TO THE FIRST EDITION (1973)

THIS BOOK was written with some haste. It seemed important to write of the Asian expulsion from Uganda and of life in the British camps before the story of the Uganda Asians became one of purely historical or academic interest. For the ordeal of the Uganda Asians is not yet over. In Uganda, the Asians who remain are still helpless victims of Amin's terror, of his desperate attempt at removing from Uganda's soil any Asian presence or enterprise. In Britain, over 4,000 Asians languish in camps, while many more, though 'resettled' in the jargon of the Uganda Resettlement Board, live on the generosity of friends and relations, supplemented by social security benefits.

In this book, I have used the words *Asian* and *Indian* interchangeably. This is because in Uganda the people of the Indian sub-continent were mostly known as Asians. Also, following popular usage in Uganda as well as in the British press, I have used the word *Uganda* both as a proper noun (indicating the name of the country) and as an adjective (as in the *Uganda* Asians). The word *citizen* in the title refers to both British and Uganda citizens. Bitter experience has taught us that in both Uganda and Britain, it has mattered little what passport we held. Our fate was determined by political and not legal factors.

I have used the word *refugee* with some hesitation. Contrary to what I believed in Uganda, a refugee is not just a person who has been displaced and has lost all or most of their possessions. A refugee is in fact more akin to a child: helpless, devoid of initiative, somebody on whom any kind of charity can be practised; in short, a totally malleable creature. A part of this book is the story of those who refused to become refugees.

In the text, I have changed all names except for those of friends and public officials. Needless to say, any similarity of characters with people living or dead is purely intentional. Also, except for statements I wrote down at official meetings with the Uganda Resettlement Board, the reproduction of all other remarks in the text are paraphrases of what was actually said. I have tried to reproduce these to the best of my memory. That these remarks have been printed here between quotation marks is purely for reasons of style and convenience. At no point did I carry pen and paper in hand.

It is customary to thank people who have played a large part in creating any work. In this case, however, I would be less than honest if I thanked those primarily responsible for this book: General Amin and the Uganda Resettlement Board.

PART ONE

1 AMIN DECREES

SATURDAY, 5 August 1972 was one of the more pleasant Kampala evenings. I had gone to dinner at the home of a university colleague. There were four of us – an African, two Arabs and myself, an Asian. The conversation centred around the change from Presidents Obote to Amin; what it implied, who had benefited, who had lost or in fact if there had been any substantive change at all. We each took turns tending to the meat which cooked on an open barbecue. The gentle heat of the fire; the cool breeze on this particularly pleasant evening; the sun, a round red ball setting in the western valley; and a hearty meal awaiting us – there was more than just a trace of satisfaction on our faces.

The university is situated on one of the nine hills that adorn Kampala, the capital city of Uganda. The hills are the residential areas for the affluent of all three races – European, Asian and African. On each hilltop is a public building: a place of worship, a school or a hospital. The central valley is where business is carried out. In one corner, between two hills, is Kampala's slum – Kisenyi. On its outer fringes Kisenyi houses the Asian and African urban poor. Within, the slum is exclusively African. In a semi-circular arc around the city are a number of exclusively African trading centres – Katwe, Wandegeya and Bwayise, expanding with time, demanding their rightful place under the sun – with an increasingly loud voice. This voice was the beginning of organised politics in Uganda in the 1940s, and it would once again echo around the city for the next three months.

But now, from where we were sitting on the university hilltop, the filth and squalor of the slum was hidden under nature's bountiful greenery. From the hilltop all seemed quiet and peaceful and beautiful.

It was eight o'clock in the evening, news time. 'Let's listen to Amin,' my host suggested. The television was switched on. There he was, a big burly he-man, addressing a gathering at the Conference Centre. The centre had been built by Obote as a venue for the Organisation of African Unity Conference, one that he never survived politically to host. It is a large and extravagant structure, and quite beautiful. This Saturday was International Cooperative Day, and so Amin addressed representatives of cooperative societies from all over Uganda. We sat down in the living room, sipping our beers and our gin and tonics, watching Amin. Life was good.

Then it came. 'The Asians must leave,' in so many words. A thunderbolt out of the blue. What could one say? Should one have expected it? Admittedly, only a year after the January 1971 coup there was a head count of Asians only. Everyone counted was issued a Green Pass. All movement was forbidden without it. In December Amin had called a special conference of Asian leaders and presented them with a list of 'Asian business malpractices'. In retrospect, all these events preceded the expulsion order, but at the time nobody expected anything so drastic to happen. Only the day before Amin had said he considered the Asians the responsibility of the British, but people just thought he was performing a series of public gestures which might prove popular and in the absence of any substantive policy.

But there was Amin again:

> *Asians came to Uganda to build the railway. The railway is finished. They must leave now...*

Why had Asians come to Uganda? When the second phase of imperialism – the late 19th century 'scramble for Africa' – began, England's main colony was India. India was said to be 'the jewel in the Imperial crown'. With it, Britain had become a fully-fledged imperial power. The territories that Britain conquered in the late 19th century all had pre-capitalist economies. There was no market for labour; commerce was secondary and peripheral; the people lived and worked on the land.

In the initial phase, when only nominal control had been established over the colonies, it was not possible to extract forced labour from the 'natives' (a practice Britain introduced at a later stage.) Labour had to be brought in from outside. For this Britain turned to its primary and most populous colony, India. Indian migration to East Africa, Mauritius, South Africa, the West Indies and Guinea began under British auspices in the late 19th century. At first Indians came as soldiers in the imperial army. Then came Indian labourers to build the railways, artisans to keep the machines working and (in some places) even peasants to work the plantations, along with petty clerks to extend administration, and finally petty traders to expand the scope of the market. Together they (the Asians) extended the horizons of the empire and built its fences.

Asians have discriminated against Africans...

The strategy of colonial rule was that an ethnically different people were used as a means of coercion in a colony. Asian soldiers assisted in the conquest of East Africa; in Uganda they entered the Kingdom of Buganda. Once Buganda had been captured, the British sought allies within the kingdom. An agreement set up in 1900 deprived the Baganda peasantry (the Baganda are the people of the Buganda province) of their land and distributed this land among a small group of chiefs who adopted the Protestant faith. Deprived of their traditional land rights, the Catholic (and later Muslim) chiefs and clan heads attempted to organise themselves politically. Rivalry between English Protestant and French Catholic missionaries and their converts ensued. Religion had thus become a political factor in Uganda.

When Buganda was secured to the British crown an army of Baganda soldiers was used to conquer Bunyoro and Toro. Prominent Baganda were later appointed as chiefs among the Bwemba. Tribalism – political conflict between tribes – became the order of the day.

There was rigid racial compartmentalisation in the newly created colonial political economy. Laws hindered Africans from entering trade and Asians from owning land. In the economy that emerged, Africans were primarily peasants and workers; Asians primarily shopkeepers, artisans and petty bureaucrats; and Europeans were bankers, wholesalers and the administrative and political elite. Race coincided with class and became politicised. Thus, in November 1971, Amin produced a list of 'Asian business malpractices,' not just 'business malpractices'.

It was not the era of independence, but that of dependence – of colonialism – that politicised race, tribe and religion in Uganda. This was the kernel of truth in the theory that colonialism rested on the basis of divide and rule.

Asians have stayed aloof. They have never mixed with Africans...

The generation of Englishmen that led the imperial assault were not racialists. Their claim to superiority was not based on their fair complexion, but on their claim to a superior ethic: the puritan ethic. They believed they had a mission: to teach the world their mode of social existence. Their puritan way of life, from their point of view, was the way of progress.

But such was not the case with their children, who were born in the colonies in privilege. Racial supremacy was their dominant ideology. It justified the continued dominance and welfare of their race at the expense of all others. And it created a rigid, racially stratified society.

Since class and race coincided in the colony, it followed that places of residence and conditions of work would also be segregated. But that was not all. Colonial life created racially distinct and exclusive ways of life. It built racially exclusive institutions for the socialisation of its future generations. I went to a government Indian secondary school, which was later integrated in 1962 – the year of independence. Our teachers were Asian with a few European supervisors. The history we learned was that of Britain and the British Empire. The literature we learned was English and Indian. The languages we leaned were English and the Indian languages of Gujarati and Urdu. After school we played at the Indian Youth League and worshipped at the Indian mosque or the Indian temple. When a number of school children wished to donate blood they were taken to the British Red Cross's Indian Blood Bank. The family, the school and the church – all racially exclusive – created three nations in one: European, Asian and African. The only knowledge and experience we held in common was that of the empire. But in the 1950s and 60s the sun was setting on the British Empire.

A racially exclusive social existence gave rise to a racial consciousness. The success of colonialism lay not just in the colonial structure we lived in, but also in the corresponding consciousness we inherited. The majority of Asians believed they were inferior to the Europeans and superior to the Africans. Most Africans believed they were inferior to both Europeans and Asians. As Frantz Fanon put it when writing of Algeria, success for colonial policy meant achieving a 'racial distribution of guilt':

> The Arab is told: 'If you are poor it is because the Jew has bled you and taken everything from you!' The Jew is told: 'You are not really of the same class as the Arab because you are white...'

> ...The Frenchman does not like the Jew, who does not like the Arab, who does not like the African.

The only significant contacts between the races were those in the market place: between seller and buyer, trader and customer, master and servant, subject and ruler. Significantly, these were all relations of power – political relationships. The equation in those times was simple.

He is an Asian; he is rich.
I am an African; I am poor.

Or

He is rich because he is Asian.
I am poor because I am African.

And this equation was substantially true.

'I have said it before that the Asians are a British responsibility...'

Unable to stand it any longer, my host switched the television off. Blank stares, expressions of disbelief. The silence was becoming intolerable. The peace and quiet of the hill was beginning to haunt me. I must go home, I thought. I wondered how my pa ents were reacting to this. I excused myself and drove home. My parents, however, were asleep. As I realised the next day, very few people were taking Amin's announcement seriously. In fact, people joked about it. Conversation centred around it for an hour or so and then it was all forgotten – but not for long. In the coming days, with the ruthlessness of a cold and efficient tactician, Amin made certain that every Asian realised the seriousness and the finality of his measure. History was in the making.

2 ORDER BEHIND CHAOS

D URING THE months of August and September it was government by broadcast in Uganda. Every evening at eight o'clock all sat glued to their television sets, if they owned one; if not they turned on the radio. A new tune signalled the beginning of the news. The lyric went: 'Farewell Asians, farewell Asians, you have milked the economy for too long...' Inevitably, the broadcast began with Amin, and just as inevitably a new decree was announced once every few days. *All Asians holding British, Indian, Pakistani and Bangladesh passports must leave.* Few took this seriously, but on 8 August Amin went ahead and signed the decree. Could he be serious? The question was written on every face.

The newspaper, the radio and the television, all of the national media, treated the decree with great seriousness. An aura of credibility was beginning to emerge. And then: *All non-citizen Asians, even those holding Kenyan and Tanzanian passports must leave.* The next evening: *Professional Asians are exempt.* Relief! I am exempt and so are most of my friends. It was incredible how this one decree drove a wedge between the non-professional and the professional in the community. All of a sudden one's identity changed from that of being an Asian to being a professional Asian. A part of the community prepared to celebrate; another to leave. But then again: *There will be no exemptions.* And finally: *All Asians, citizens or not, must leave.*

This last decree was Amin's clearest and most sincere statement. He wanted Uganda rid of all Asians, even the 23,242 that had been recorded as citizens in the Asian census of 1971.

Among the Asian community, mass depression set in. It did not matter that, as a result of pressures from within and without, Amin had decided to let citizen Asians stay. All it meant was that he was learning the political importance of legal camouflage. He would now simply change tactics: somehow pronounce these Asians non-citizens and make them leave with the rest.

Uganda Argus

Kampala, August, 1972

5 August

THE FUTURE OF ASIANS IN UGANDA

It will be Britain's responsibility

PRESIDENT AMIN will ask the British Government to take over responsibility of all Asians in Uganda who are holding British passports because they are sabotaging the economy of the country.

7 August

Asians milked the cow: They did not feed it
– Gen. Amin

PRESIDENT AMIN has disclosed that he would summon the British High Commissioner to Uganda to make arrangements and remove the 80,000 Asian British passport holders within three months.

9 August

Ugandans hail move on Asians
IT WAS OVERDUE, SAY AFRICANS: 'GOOD LUCK' SAY THE ASIANS

CABINET BACKS PRESIDENT'S DECISION

10 August

Three months to quit – except those in essential jobs
Some will stay, some will go

18 August

African traders to show support to Gen Amin

THE UGANDA African Traders Associaiton will hold a public proecession in Kampala tomorrow in support of President Amin's move to expel British Asians and to declare the 'economic war'.

18 August

'We shall suffer for sometime, but it does not matter'
EXEMPTION CLAUSE DELETED

24 August

ALL ASIANS MUST GO

President's new phase in the 'economic war'

PRESIDENT IDI Amin said at the weekend that all the 23,000 Asians who hold Uganda citizenship will also have to leave the country, in addition to the 60,000 who have already been ordered to quit.

PROFESSIONAL BRITISH Aisans who were previously exempted from the expulsion orders will also be asked to leave Uganda 'because they cannot serve the country with good spirit after the departure of other Asians'. And refugees now in Uganda will soon be returned to their respective countries.

Excerpts from the Uganda Argus

So all citizen Asians were asked to come and queue up at the Immigration Office and verify their citizenship claim. Proper 'documentary evidence' had to be presented. This meant that besides passports, the birth and marriage certificates of both the individuals concerned and their parents must be produced. A process of summarily invalidating citizenships began. If your father was born in East Africa and was over 50 years old, he was most unlikely to have a birth certificate at all. You were then said to have 'insufficient documentary evidence' and your claim to Uganda citizenship was declared false. In many cases half the family were declared stateless and the other half Ugandans. The Ugandans then inevitably 'lost' their passports or a document, and joined their relations in the bulging ranks of the stateless. In a few days this process produced thousands of stateless refugees, all more or less arbitrarily rendered so.

The decrees, however, did not stop there. Every day saw the announcement of another formality to be undergone, a new form to be filled in, one more law to be observed. Initially it all seemed irrational. Later, however, one got to the point of it all. Faced with expulsion in three months and a limit of £50 on the assets each family could expatriate, the affluent were making every attempt to salvage as many of their assets as possible, by any means possible. The normal practices of large businesses – that of under-invoicing exports and over-invoicing imports, and then sharing the difference in foreign currency with the overseas importer or exporter – were now out of the question. The government knew about it and kept a keen and watchful eye over all transactions.

Ingenious means were improvised. Someone would buy a ticket from Sabena or BOAC to go ten or 20 times around the world. The international corporations could take the money out, so people planned to get refunds for their tickets once they were outside Uganda. If not refunds, then at least they could extend or just use the tickets. At least they would have something in return for their existing assets. As rumours in the city had it, three million shillings (approximately £175,000) worth of tickets had been sold in a week. At the end of the week the government announced that no one could buy a ticket which took them from Uganda to more than one destination, i.e. only a simple ticket to one place with no stopovers could now be purchased. Furthermore, the buying of any travel tickets had to be endorsed by the Bank of Uganda.

The affluent then turned to other measures. Simple things like just driving into Kenya in an expensive car were soon outlawed. The resourceful, however, persisted. Non-existent cars were registered in Kenya and number-plates mailed to Uganda. The cars, now with a Kenya registration, were easily driven across the border.

Amin was forced to contend with a shrewd and experienced business community. He had to make certain that in the two months or so remaining to them, the businessmen could not also take with them a large part of their assets, thereby defeating his policy. (Thus the decree that no business was allowed to stay open after tax clearance.) If Amin was to succeed, it was necessary that he create sufficient disorder to make it impossible for any businessman to pursue a consistent policy in expatriating funds. Thus the endless decrees. At the same time he had to maintain sufficient order to make possible an exodus; and most important, not to give an excuse to any external power, particularly Britain, to intervene militarily in defence of 'her citizens.' This he achieved with remarkable success.

The harassment continued; in fact it accelerated and went far beyond the announcing of decrees. The most extraordinary event was a presidential visit to army training camps, as officially explained in the *Uganda Argus*, 'to examine possible areas where camps could be set up to accommodate non-citizen Asians, who without specific exemption by the government would not have removed themselves from Uganda by the deadline of 8 November 1972'. Arbitrary arrests of Asians followed this visit.

To understand the physical harassment of Asians and the officially perpetuated fear of an impending reign of terror, one must turn to the actions of the British high commission in Kampala. The function of the British high commisions in Uganda and the rest of East Africa ever since the 1968 act of the British parliament which created different classes of British passport holders had been to stem the tide of British Asians wishing to emigrate to Britain. Its staff contended with long queues of potential Asian émigrés, responded to hostile criticism from the Ugandan and Asian press, or simply remained calm while Asians demonstrated outside and inside the mission. The few years since 1968 had trained them not to be the proverbially cheerful and accommodating mission staff, but the indifferent and tough guards around the castle that was Britain. Their character and training were quite suited to following the sort of directives that would now come from their masters, the British government, who certainly were not to be convinced by any number of speeches or announcements that the gates of the castle must now be opened before a flood of coloured immigrants.

In the months of August and September, when thousands of people streamed into the city from the country and hundreds daily queued in front of the British high commission, sleeping there night after night, the high commission stayed open only from 10 in the morning to 12.30, and again from 2 until 4.30 in the afternoon for five days a week. It was as if they were playing a gentlemanly game of cricket! During this time, the Ugandan government offices stayed open from 7am till 7pm, seven days a week. It was clear to all of us – and must have been to Amin as well – that he could do anything to the Asians, short of killing them all, and still have

Uganda Asians reach out for application forms outside
the offices of the British high commission in Kampala,
15 August 1972

little impact on the high commission. They simply would not open their
doors beyond the conventional hours and just would not work at a pace
not befitting a gentleman.

Finally, Amin realised that the only measures that would work would
be measures against white British subjects. He instructed his army to go
out into the streets and arbitrarily arrest the first 100 British citizens they
came across. The effect was electric. Only three days after these arrests
the high commission was galvanised into action. Its doors opened from
7am to 7pm, and it was announced that additional staff would soon be
hired to cope with the large number of Asian applicants. His purpose ac-
complished, Amin now released all the Britons who had been gaoled.

These arrests had received considerable prominence in the British
press, which we read every Sunday morning in Kampala.

It described in detail these 'atrocities' and cited them as convin ing proof that the presidency of Uganda was occupied by a madman. To us, that sounded quite ludicrous. It was clear that a game of nerves was being played out between Amin and the British high commission. The Asians had simply become one collective political football, which each side tried to kick into the other's goal. Not having scored by committing atrocities against Asians, Amin had simply changed tactics. Once he substituted white Britons for Asians, he succeeded.

Such was the context in which emerged the terror campaign of Amin's army against the Asians. While terror was initially designed to achieve a specific political goal, pressurising the high commission into granting entry visas to the expelled Asians, it soon became the weapon of the rank-and-file soldiers intent upon seizing this opportunity for private greed. For Amin's army was largely made of fresh recruits; it was not a disciplined force.

The first group of Asians to leave Uganda were those that went to India. From Kampala they took a train to the Kenyan port of Mombasa where a ship was to take them to Bombay. Letters from them told of being stopped on the way by bands of Ugandan soldiers, of all their belongings being taken, of the men made to lie down on the ground while the women were raped. From the countryside news gradually filtered into the city telling of individual Asians who had been kidnapped by soldiers, of fam-ilies who paid fortunes for the return of the male members and of other families who lost their father or brothers because they had no money to pay a ransom.

As the situation deteriorated, the city, which had to date been im-mune to such extremes, got a taste of armed greed. A familiar pattern emerged: business owners were charged with hoarding money, stripped of whatever cash they had on the premises and, in a number of cases, thrown into the boots of army cars – where they usually suffocated to death – before being thrown out a few miles from the city into the bush.

The theft of Asian property, even during the most chaotic times, followed an established pattern. Everything that the Asians had to leave behind was guarded carefully by army and police officials. Any potential looters were shot dead upon sight and without hesitation. Amin's orders were that the Asians' property was to be guarded as ruthlessly as the Asians themselves were being expelled. The same material interest was at stake in both cases. For it was clear that once the Asians had departed

LONDON Tuesday 29th August 1972

DAILY EXPRESS

*1,000 STORM HIGH COMMISSION AS
THE BIG ENTRY-PAPERS RUSH STARTS*

Chaos as Asians scramble

Kampala

ASIANS WAVING passports pushed and shouted as they struggled to be first into the centre, which opened today to deal with those waiting to go to Britain.

British passport officials had invited 200 people with entry vouchers to call and complete their processing. The identifying number on each voucher was read out earlier on radio and TV.

But when the doors of the centre opened at 8 a.m. there were nearly 1,000 people in the queue. Some had been waiting in the rain since 4 a.m.

Those at the back of the queue began pushing and shouting, forcing the mass of people against the plate-glass windows.

Police were called in and took nearly and hour to restore order. One official said: "It was madness. Sheer chaos."

Text: © Express Sydication 1972

a large part of their businesses, homes and cars would be legitimately acquired by the high army brass.

It was here that the conflict of interests emerged between the army officials and its rank and file. For the soldiers realised that when the time came for the legal allocation of Asian homes and businesses, the sun would only shine on high-ranking officials. If ordinary soldiers were to share in the spoils, their only opportunity to do so was before the Asians departed – and for this they had necessarily to resort to illegal means.

Seen in this context, what happened in Uganda during the 90 days begins to acquire another meaning. For those Britons who care to read their own history it will be a familiar one. When speaking of England, Marx describes this process as 'the primitive accumulation of capital,' a set of events 'written in the annals of mankind in letters of blood and fire'. In England this process took a different form: embezzlement of church funds, robbery on the high seas and the expulsion of peasants from the land. In Uganda, it has meant the embezzlement of state funds, robbery on the highways and the expulsion of the Asians. To other specifically English forms, slavery and colonial plunder, there are no parallels in Uganda – at least not yet.

With the passing of days, the city closed at dusk. People took to indoor entertainment, to restaurants and to afternoon cinema shows. At night the city assumed a ghostly and deserted look. Although fear was written on every face, its articulation was verboten. But hard as we tried to maintain this imposed gaiety of bars and cinema-houses, every once in a while, the collective tension, suppressed to a limit, would burst out in a single expression.

One Sunday afternoon two friends and I sat in a theatre watching an Indian film. It was a romantic musical, as most Indian films tend to be. Towards the middle of it we suddenly heard loud and angry voices from the balcony. As if possessed of one soul, the audience rose. In the midst of the shrieks, one could hear shouts: 'The army is here.' In a few minutes the theatre was empty. The audience, a part of it standing outside, the rest running in all directions, gradually realised that there was no army in fact. It was only a quarrel that had broken out between two people in the balcony.

Gradually, a primitive racial solidarity emerged out of a common racial predicament. The public events, Amin's terror campaign and the stubborn intransigence of the British high commission merely underlined what every Asian had become painfully aware of through personal experiences those last 90 days: the fact of colour and its enormous political implications. What was important was not that one held a British or Ugandan passport, but the colour of one's skin. British or Ugandan, an Asian was an Asian in the eyes of both the British and Ugandan authorities.

One afternoon in October I was having tea with a British friend and colleague in the university senior common room. John was a visiting lecturer from an English university. The conversation centred on what my father could do for a living in England.

'What about importing things from Uganda, say timber?' John suggested.

I shrugged my shoulders.

'Seriously, it is in considerable demand in England. I wonder what the import duties on it would be.'

Once again I shrugged my shoulders.

'Well, why don't we go to the British high commission and find out?' he persisted.

I looked at him in wonder. The British high commission had, for the past month, been besieged by a large number of Asians. The largest mission in Kampala, the high commission has a shaded courtyard that can easily seat over 200 people. However, the Asians who queued at the high commission – sleeping through the night, standing in the daytime, with nothing but newspapers to shield them from the rain or shine, without food or drinks to relieve their discomfort – were never allowed to make use of this courtyard. Instead, in the first few weeks of the expulsion, they were herded to a side entrance where one room had been converted into the passport office. The front entrance was carefully guarded by security officers. No Asian was allowed in. All were sent to the passport section, regardless of the nature of their business. And now John wanted to go to the high commission and inquire about the import duty for Ugandan timber!

But off we went. There was the usual crowd and the usual security guards. With his face unshaven, his hair uncombed and uncut for at least a few months, a Trotsky moustache, horn-rimmed glasses and a slightly dirty undershirt as his upper garment, John hardly looked the picture of a respectable, establishment type. Nonetheless he walked on confidently. As he reached the door, the guard opened it, almost as if he had been expected. I followed, a little timidly. The guard gave me a searching look but John chided, 'He's with me.' Open Sesame! I was in. The Asians outside looked at me. 'He must be important,' their faces seemed to say. It took precisely ten minutes for the secretary to get us into the commercial section, for the attaché to get his secretary to do a little research in the library and for us to be armed with not only statistics on import duty but also names and addresses of timber merchants in and around London. There had been no questions, no suggestions that we make an appointment, no wait, no queue, not even an inquiring look. As we came out, I said to John, 'How does it feel to be white?' He didn't hear me and I decided not to press the point. But I learned something that afternoon.

A few days later, I had a date with some friends. We went to the Copper Bar in the Grand Hotel. In colonial days it was known as the Imperial Hotel and was exclusively for whites. It is rather like an American bar, small, dark and, in normal circumstances, noisy. This evening, the customers were primarily African and British. Apart from the three of us, there was only one other group of Asians, all of us quietly drinking and thinking of our respective problems. In marked contrast to us were the Britons, laughing, joking and loud, while emptying their beer mugs. There seemed an almost total abandonment in their laughter. Jagdish, one of my friends who had been looking at them ever since we came in, suddenly turned around. 'Look at them, laughing, confident. They are not worried. They know they have a powerful government behind them.' There was a trace of resentment in his voice.

3   ASIAN RESPONSES

A PASSPORT is essentially a class document. People whose resources and opportunities are so limited that they cannot even conceive of travelling beyond a few miles of their home have no passport. Nearly 90 per cent of the African people of Uganda fall into this category. And a sizable minority of Asians – small rural shopkeepers who said they would rather die than leave the country and the lowest paid of the artisans and workers in the urban areas – also belonged to this segment of society. A pass-port to them was an exotic document, a plaything of the affluent. The sudden turn of events, the rather cruel entry of politics into their personal lives, left them utterly bewildered. The first few that attempted to come down to the city were robbed on the way by members of the armed forces. Those who stayed behind became targets of organised army raids. The response was to stay put.

Eventually a voluntary committee was formed of urban Asians and sympathetic university-based Britons. Together they organised caravans with police escorts, and these unfortunate rural Asians were brought to the city. A few lucky ones found distant relations who put them up. Others were taken care of by charitable organisations in temples and mosques. They began to emulate the city labourers and artisans who went to the high commission with all their belongings, spent a number of nights waiting, and finally got in – only to be chucked out because they had no documents. One of them, who had tried to get a number of my friends to read him the city newspaper and was trying to make sense of what was going on said to me: 'When the British came to Uganda they didn't bring any passports. Why do we need them?' I told him the British had guns and we did not. The next time I saw him, he had ended up, together with others in the same predicament, in the same Sikh temple which the United Nations had converted into a refugee camp for the stateless. From there they headed for more permanent UN camps in Malta, Spain, Austria and Belgium, victims of circumstances they neither controlled nor understood.

Not everybody was adversely affected by Amin's expulsion order. Particularly happy were those who had long been making attempts to emigrate to Britain but had been held up by the quota voucher system. This group comprised two categories of people. The first were small-scale urban traders and lower-level civil servants. They were both victims of 'Africanisation' in commerce and the civil service, a policy followed with increasing vigour since the 1950s when the British initiated it after a series of urban riots and African demands for greater participation in the urban economy. The majority of these had applied for Uganda passports but had not been granted them. (As the Obote talks with the Home Office in 1970 showed, besides over 20,000 Asians who were already citizens, there were over 30,000 who had applied for Uganda passports. But their applications had not yet been processed.) Over the years many had their work permits cancelled by the government on the grounds that they were foreigners. At the same time, the British high commission refused to grant them entry visas into England. They became victims of a 'working arrangement' between the British and Ugandan authorities. The Ugandans, while cancelling their work permits, kept on granting them innumerable two-month 'visitor's visas'. The British could then safely keep them waiting in the queue. They lived off their savings, and once these were exhausted, off charity. As time went on they became increasingly militant, staged loud and sometimes violent demonstrations in front of the high commission, but the British remained unimpressed and unmoved. From their point of view, there was no difference between a government that was determined to get rid of one race among its citizens (the Uganda Asians) and a government that was just as determined to keep outside of its borders the same racial category of citizens (the British Asians).

To those poor people Amin was a hero who had, with one mighty stroke, opened the gates of Britain for one and all.

The second category of people that stood in the queues were well-to-do professionals and newly prosperous traders. Frightened of the possibility of a left-wing government that would nationalise, or a right-wing government that would Africanise, they wanted to get out with all their newly created wealth. The expulsion order, with one clean sweep, ended the old era of the queue system. The same decree, however, also stipulated that no family could take out more than £50 in cash. These people, though, having anticipated getting emigration vouchers in a year or two, had already established London bank accounts and had sent some of their savings out. Their losses nonetheless were real. The responsibility for their misfortune lay not with President Amin and his expulsion order, but with the British government and its quota system.

The largest group of people to share the same fate were those on more or less fixed incomes and who previously were not immediately facing the threat of Africanisation: middle-level civil servants and traders, marginally well-off artisans and workers. They were people who knew that to live in the country would not be possible for them unless they became a part of it. They had consciously chosen to reject Duncan Sandys' pre-independence offer of British citizenship and had instead registered as Uganda citizens immediately after independence. But now they found, as they stood in queues to verify their citizenship, that their passports were being torn up or stamped invalid one after another.

To understand their misfortune it is necessary to understand their social circumstances. The only fixed income group among the Asians, they had become the staunchest converts to a puritan commercial ethic. This was, in part, also a result of the peculiarly colonial social conditions. In a society where a *racial* consciousness was highly developed, the social contacts of these people were not with others of their own class, but with others of their own race, and therefore with people more prosperous than themselves. Within these ranks, the stigma of failure was the worst form of discrimination a person could face. The standards they set themselves were not the standards of their own class but the standards of another class, a more prosperous class. Their heroes were self-made men, and these were real people. They were those who had started out without a penny and had risen through the ranks of the civil service or trade. But such success stories were fewer after the 1950s. Saving was becoming increasingly difficult for the less affluent, especially for the lower middle class and particularly for Asians in this stratum because in colonial Uganda laws stipulated that non-Africans (and with a very small resident European community, 'non-African' was inevitably a euphemism for Asians) could not buy land outside specified township areas. As demand exceeded the limited supply, prices of rents rocketed. The landlord, an Asian, made exorbitant profit from the tenant, also an Asian.

As time went on and living became more expensive, families like these had further to tighten their belts to accumulate savings. Parents confined themselves to two meals a day instead of three. The wife bought only one sari a year. The children did not see any films. The elder child worked while the younger child would typically be the one to be educated, obtain a degree and thus be in a position to tap opportunities that evaded all others in the family. One thus had families who had saved over the course of 15, 20, even 30 years something in the order of 20,000 to 40,000 shillings (£1,000 to £2,000).

With the expulsion order the Uganda Asians became stateless and with the £50 limit on transferable assets, their savings vanished. These, however, were the savings of a lifetime. While every other class of people gave way to conspicuous and incessant consumption in the final two months, this class persisted in its old ways. Prisoners of habits they had learned from material necessity, they knew no other way of life. To squander the savings of a lifetime would be the ultimate sin. Perhaps God will answer our prayers, perhaps the UN will get us compensation for our assets, perhaps Amin will give us our citizenship back – perhaps. Those who were once determined to make their own fate were now leaving all they had made to fate.

It was amongst this group that I found the most tragic cases. One afternoon I went down to see my old secondary school teacher. We had maintained contact over the years when I had gone abroad to study. He had continued with his teaching job, living in a government subsidised house.

He served me tea, according to Indian custom. I asked him if I could help.

'Nobody can help me, Mahmood. I am 60 now. In a few years I was going to retire. I would then receive a pension, and with the 20,000 shillings I have saved I thought I wouldn't be a burden on anyone. Now, there'll be no savings and no pensions. I am not young. But, I have many students in England, Mahmood. If I am in trouble, I am sure they'll help me. Will you leave me your address?'

As he was talking, an old lady came in. She could have been anywhere between 50 and 60, I thought.

'I have been looking for you Masterji,' she said, 'One never knows these days who's gone and who is still behind. They say I'll be sent to England with my children, all six of them. You know the eldest, Manu. He is 18 but still in school. I wish he were alive [referring to her husband]. They say England is very cold, and nobody there bothers about anybody else. God, what will I do? I don't even speak English. But I can cook and sew. As long as there's work. But you will help me, Masterji, won't you? God bless you, Masterji.' ('Master' refers to a teacher, '-ji' is a suffix that connotes endearment and respect.)

Masterji looked at me and then at her, 'Yes, I'll help you,' he said softly. She left. There was little else to be said. I finished my tea, declined his offer of another cup and said I'd come back another time.

I thought I had seen the bottom when I was speaking to Masterji. But in those days in Kampala every bottom was a false one. I began to think I was living in, or at least staring into, what seemed a bottomless pit. Aimlessly, I had been driving through the streets of old Kampala, past the old secondary school, around Museum Hill where Captain Lugard had won the crucial Battle of Mengo and had begun the colonial history of Uganda, down by the police station and through the small houses of the lower middle class Asians and then up the hill to the university, Makerere. But, before I could go round the roundabout and begin the incline to the university, a familiar hand was waving at me. I stopped the car. It was Sushila.

Sushila was the younger sister of a friend, brought up in an extremely orthodox, tradition-bound family where women are always supposed to 'know their place'. Years ago, when she was in secondary school and doing fairly well, the question came up: why not send her to university? Certainly the family could afford it. But no, the father would have none of this, 'The modern world will not come into my house.' And the father always had the last word. Sushila's life had been mapped out. Its highlights would be an arranged marriage and then a number of children. That was four years ago. Since then, I had only seen her once.

'Well, I thought you may be gone by now, even married. What is happening?'

'A lot is happening, brother. Would you believe it, I am going to Canada.'

'What!' I had totally betrayed my shock.

She laughed. 'Yes, I know. You said you expected me to be married. Thank God I resisted that for the last two yeas. Now my parents are going to England. The family has a little money there, but too little. They cannot pay a good dowry for me. So, I'm free. And what is more, the Canadians offered me not just an entry visa but also a scholarship.'

'Come on, let's go and celebrate. We'll have some tea,' I suggested.

'No, I can't. I have to say goodbye to my Masterji. God knows if I'll ever see him again.' She couldn't make up her mind whether to look sad or happy. I laughed.

I resumed my drive, now heading for the university, the words of a young Ugandan poet ringing in my ear.

The sun is not always dead at night And fire doesn't always beget ash...

The next day was Sunday. I went in the morning to the Popular Book Supply, the one bookshop that sold the Sunday edition of British papers. I found there a queue of over a hundred people. In September and October, if one wanted to meet an Asian friend, the thing to do was to go visit five places: the Bank of Uganda, the British high commission, the Canadian high commission, Uganda immigration or the tax office, and look through the people who had lined up there. In the city, there was neither business as usual, nor pleasure as usual. The queues began early in the morning, around 4 am and went on till 7 in the evening. In October, the Asians' queue at the bank was joined by Kenyan African workers, afraid that they might be the next to be expelled. In the days before the Amin coup, faced with an increasingly militant working class, Obote had expelled Kenya workers en masse. Their problem was not just that they were few in number and came from a neighbouring African country, but also that they were solely working class. The world little noticed their plight. They were news for a day and then they were forgotten.

These thoughts were interrupted by my getting to the front of the newspaper queue. '*Observer*, please.' I scanned the paper. The first of the Asians were arriving in Britain and the paper carried interviews with them. There was one simple theme in it: the loss of property. I felt a sense of rage swell up within me. This was the time of the British high commission dragging its feet in processing entry visas and the subsequent physical harassment of Asians by the Uganda authorities. The interviews contained not a word about it.

The first of the Asians to leave Uganda were from amongst the wealthiest: the ex-cotton ginners who had become the industrialists and wholesale traders, and the few doctors and lawyers who had extremely lucrative practices. Those among them who most feared government investigation into their affairs were the first to leave, or rather, flee. These were the people who had long had overseas bank accounts, who made certain that one member of their family was a Uganda citizen and another a British citizen. Though a small minority in number, probably as small as those who had no passports, they were politically the most significant

© PA/PA Archive/Press Association

Some of the first expelled Uganda Asians arrive in Britain, 18 September 1972

Asians in Uganda, for they were the bourgeois 'who had milked the cow'. In a racially stratified economy, however, they were known as the 'Asian capitalists' and not just as capitalists. But it would be wrong to think that the capitalists in Uganda were even primarily Asians. The Asian capitalists were few – the most important ones being Madhvani and Mehta, both owning important manufacturing and agricultural enterprises in Uganda, Kenya and India. The overwhelming majority of Asian businessmen, however, were merchants, operating in the commercial sector, heavily indebted to the banks. A study conducted in 1968 showed that approximately 80 per cent of the total commercial bank assets in Uganda were controlled by three banks, Barclays Bank DCO, The National and Grindlays Bank and the Standard Bank – all British. The other foreign banks, the Netherlands Bank, Ottoman Bank, Habib Bank, Bank of Baroda and Bank of India, controlled another 10 per cent. The remaining 10 per cent was controlled by the Bank of Uganda and the Uganda Commercial Bank. In October, when Asian businesses started closing down en masse, one could walk down the main streets of Kampala and see signs such as 'Property of Barclays Bank DCO,' or 'Property of the Standard Bank' on locked up Asian businesses. It seemed clear that unless Amin moved against it, the primary beneficiary of the Asian expulsion would be British capital, not African. British control was also very important in other sectors: insurance, the plantation industry and wholesale trade. In sum the 'commanding heights of the economy' (a phrase often used in Uganda during those days and referring to finance capital – i.e. banking and insurance) were controlled by the British, not the Asians. The Asians had been intermediaries. The masters, as had been the case since 1900, were still the British. With the departure of the Asians, Amin would quickly realise this.

Absorbed in my fury, I shut the paper and started walking along the street towards town. A familiar voice came from behind me. 'Ah, I know what you are so upset about. Bastards, aren't they? Most of us have five senses. These people have only one – the sense of property. Come, let's have a drink and forget about it all.' It was Jagdish, and with him Malik. We went to a nearby hotel and ordered three beers. For a few minutes we talked, and then just as suddenly, the conversation died. Each was

---

DAILY EXPRESS

Amin's 'free for all'

No cash needed when Africans want to buy an Asian's home or business

Kampala

GOOD TIMES for Uganda Africans who want to take over the homes and firms of departing Asians were forecast by President Amin and one of his Ministers today.

First, General Amin told a meeting of British and other bank managers in Kampala:—

"Banks should have no excuse whatever for not lending to traders and business men who demonstrate their dedication, efficiency, and integrity. Banks are expected to contribute towards the economic war by assisting African business men."

General Amin, wearing full-dress uniform and carrying a baton, said foreign investors should invest in Uganda only through black Ugandans.

preoccupied with his own problems. I looked at Jagdish, this man who was so different from most other people I knew.

Jagdish came from a poor family. He had just finished secondary education when his father died. Despite being the youngest brother, he volunteered to work and put his two brothers through college, at the same time supporting his mother and sister. His work was teaching in a private school for the children of farmers on the outskirts of the city. In Uganda, the government-run schools are the best equipped and the most sought after. Private schools are financed by the parents of children who have been rejected elsewhere, operating on a limited budget with a small and poorly paid staff. His dedication as a teacher and his interest in his students led him to fraternise with families – farmers and soldiers. He got to know them, like them and understand them. Gradually he began to spend his leisure time in African areas on the outskirts of the city, frequenting bars that were in fact miniature political discussion groups in the 1960s.

Jagdish was one of the few people I knew who was not trapped by the social conditions he was born into, who had successfully risen above his social environment to be able to see its limitations. He revolted against the perverse nature of the society around him, especially the affluent Asian society, with its almost totally privatised existence and increasingly conspicuous consumption. His life, in contrast to that of others, knew no barriers of race or class.

In the late 1960s, when Jagdish met Malik, who had been an administrator with the American embassy and had saved some money, he persuaded him to rent some rooms and start a school for the children of the farmers. Now he could realise his dreams and have his own school. Its staff and students would be multi-racial, its subject matter would be stripped of colonial content.

When Jagdish found out he had to leave, his immediate concern was to make certain the school would not collapse on his departure, for he was the headmaster, the history teacher and the substitute teacher in case one of the staff was absent. He set about training one of the African teachers, Mugoba, in the mechanics of running the school. Every morning students would ask Jagdish when he was leaving. He would remain quiet. One day he did not go to school. Instead he queued outside the British high commission to get his passport stamped. Mugoba took charge. The students demanded Jagdish's presence. When that failed they took it out on Mugoba, beat him up and refused to either leave or behave. A few days later, Jagdish left for London. He told me not to go back to the school, for he did not ever want to talk about it.

But before then, as he and Malik and I sat sipping our drinks, I wondered what was going on in his mind. He was a third generation Ugandan, and had never left the country. For the first time in his life he was doing what he wanted to do, and that for a reasonable income. How did he feel?

'What are you thinking of, Jagdish?'

'You may not believe it, Mahmood. But sometimes, when you lose everything, you feel a sense of freedom.'

4 AMIN AND AFRICAN REACTION

SOCIAL CONTACTS between Uganda Africans and Asians were restricted to the rich and the poor; among the former out of expediency, among the latter as the result of necessity. For the vast majority of Asians, personal contacts with Africans were limited to relations either with domestic servants or with business and administrative associates. After the expulsion order the African administrators remained, as always, polite but indifferent. The daily ritual of having to wade through lengthy red tape meant that every Asian came in frequent contact with officialdom, particularly with administrators. It was a tedious affair. One waited for hours, with the tropical sun above and the scorched pavement below.

At the Uganda immigration office, where I stood in line with a hundred others, the officials had decided to check people's documents before they got to the counter, so those with a missing document might be saved a number of hours of waiting. A very humane gesture. One of the officials, a rather amiable man, was briskly going through my part of the queue. He stopped to examine my neighbour's documents. After the usual greeting the neighbour unexpectedly asked:

'So you think we milked the cow but didn't feed it?' repeating Amin's oft-quoted charge against Asians.

The fellow looked up and smiled.

'If you think that is the whole story, you are not only wrong but in trouble,' my neighbour continued.

The official looked up, a question on his face.

My neighbour persisted. 'Do you know what an Asian would do if he were in your place?'

Silence.

'Do you see this queue of people?' 'Yes.'

'And the cruel sun?' 'Yes.'

'And how uncomfortable these people are?'

'Yes,' but now the official was becoming a bit impatient.

'If I were in your place, I'd have a stand of Coca-Cola out there, pay somebody to sell the cokes and maybe some groundnuts, and make myself some money.' Everybody in the queue laughed. The official smiled good-naturedly.

The next day, when I returned to the queue, I saw a stand of Coca-Cola, and a small queue in front of it! It was the birth of an African businessman.

In the early days of September the vast majority of the population, so far as one could tell, remained indifferent. Reactions to Amin's decree came from the politically conscious classes: traders, workers and students.

The first signs of jubilation and support for Amin's decree came from the African trading centres around Kampala, particularly Katwe and Wandegeya. These centres were also the birthplace of the first African shopkeeping class in Uganda.

Compared to the peasant who tilled his own piece of land and developed relations with relatively few people, the emergence of the trader was in itself a political event. His shop became a meeting place for farmers and lorry drivers in the area. The lorry drivers transported the cotton and coffee of the inland farmers to Asian and European ginners and hullers and became the one channel through which the grievances of urban and rural Africans were communicated back and forth. (After all, it was the lorry and the taxi drivers who had organised the first strike in Uganda's history.) The trader's shop became a marketplace of ideas where individual grievances were gradually shaped into collective demands. His work gave the trader the aptitude for organising both things and people. In time, the trader found compatriots and gradually there emerged a small African shopkeeping class. The major hindrance to its growth was the fact that these were not the first traders in the area, even in the rural areas. The Asians were better established and more competitive. The two fought bitterly over the right to exist. Once again, conflict of class interests appeared as racial conflict.

The African business class emerged in the 1930s, consolidated itself in the 1940s, and in the 1950s launched Uganda's first nationwide political organisation. The event that marked this was a widely and successfully organised trade boycott of rural Asian shopkeepers, lasting over a year. No wonder this class was the first to proclaim Amin's expulsion order as progress on the march. They were the only ones to spontaneously march in acclamation of the expulsion decree. Admittedly, the numbers at these marches never exceeded a thousand. The low figures, however, were not a measure of their support for Amin but, rather, testimony to the organisational weakness of this class, a weakness that allowed for the strength of Amin's own personality.

Among the working class, although there were no public expressions of support for Amin, class hostility towards the Asians came to the surface. For those Asians who were not employers – and that meant for the great majority – this hostility was confined to public places like restaurants. In a pre-industrial society like Uganda, market relationships are very much patron– client relationships. There exists not just a formal business, but also an informal social relation between the shopkeeper, the restaurant owner, or the waiter and their respective customers. The waiter was now far more formal with his Asian customers. Sometimes the Asian was just ignored for a while, occasionally there was even a plain refusal to serve him.

Among the more organised sections of the working class the hostility was manifested in a more organised fashion. In the sugar plantations owned by Madhvani, the rich Asian magnate, workers went on strike. Interestingly enough, the government sent in troops compelling the workers to return to their jobs. The government maintained that strikes were not necessary. The plantation would soon be owned by an African businessman. The class basis of Amin's decree was gradually becoming apparent.

Hostility, however, was far from more obvious among small African businessmen. One evening, on my way to the university, I stopped at Wandegeya, where there are many African retail shops. I went into the shop I had always gone to and asked the lady, with whom I was on cordial terms by now, for a packet of cigarettes. We talked a little as she handed them to me. Just as she was getting the change, a youngish fellow in his mid-20s came to the counter, stared at me and said in Swahili, 'Why are you still here?' I understood exactly what he meant, but pretended ignorance. When I still did not respond he shouted it out and banged his fist on the counter for emphasis. At this point the lady in the shop stepped forward and said, 'I don't want to have a fight in my shop.' I was amazed at her emphasis on my shop and not on my safety. Looking around I realised that a small crowd had gathered around us. For the first time I felt like a foreigner in this country, my home, and the whole weight of the events of the past few months suddenly sank into me. Staring into my face was the malice of class hatred. One single emotion gripped my whole being: fear.

I ran across the street and to the car. Fortunately, the traffic blocked off everyone else who ran behind me. Once inside the car, I drove as fast as I could to the sanctuary of the university, ran up the stairs and into the flat of a friend, sat down and had a drink.

The University had traditionally been a centre of left-wing activity. The coup that had overthrown Obote had secured strong support from the British government. In the first year of the second republic the British high commission, at least publicly, occupied the position of a de facto advisor to Amin. Students saw Amin as no more than an agent of British capital. His actions against the Asian business community turned this hostility into ambivalence. The student newspaper, *The Makererean*, put it quite clearly and courageously. Amin's expulsion of Asians could be a prelude to the formation of either a socialist Uganda or a black Ugandan bourgeoisie. If Amin opted for the former, he must nationalise 'the commanding heights of the economy' controlled by British capital, and he would have complete student support. On the other hand, if Amin was only playing bandmaster for African business, then Amin and Makerere must part ways.

As time went on, it became clear that Amin had opted for the second alternative and that his target was only Asian business. In fact, he went on to announce the expulsion of all Asians, citizen or not. At this time the National Union of Students of Uganda (NUSU) was holding its annual convention. The central committee invited Amin to address them on the final night. As he rose to speak placards loudly proclaimed, 'We oppose all forms of racism.' The president of NUSU, Kasimba Masiko, rose and presented Amin with a memorandum. It plainly stated student opposition to the expulsion of Asian citizens. This was the first sign of public opposition to Amin.

Concerned that he was not receiving student support, in the next week, Amin called a rally in City Square of all students from both the university and the high schools. The media announced that the University Student Guild (the university-wide organisation of all students) had invited Amin to speak to them. At the university, however, orders had been given that all students must report to their halls of residence after lunch, and then march to City Square in formation. On a generous estimate, a little over half the student body attended. I remember going there curious as to what the man would do. The afternoon heat was particularly severe, and we had to wait for over an hour. About that time an army jeep roared up. Nobody realised that its driver was Amin. It was taken for granted that the president would come in a chauffeur-driven limousine, at least a Mercedes-Benz. At the first sign of recognition, the crowd of onlookers, non-university Africans, roared approval. Amin stepped out, the same he-man I had seen on television. Dressed in battle fatigues, gun dangling at his side, he stood there, facing the students, waiting for the ovation that never came. Though surprised, they seemed hostile. Certainly they were quiet.

This was the first time I heard Amin in person. He was reading from a prepared text. It sounded most uninspiring and he clearly lacked confidence. He spoke haltingly. It was quite clear that he did not know much English and that he had not written the speech himself. He was followed by the president of the student guild, Tumusiime Mutebile, who, in the presence of foreign journalists, calmly stated the students' demand: the expulsion of Asian businessmen must lead to further nationalisations, not to black private enterprise. The gathering ended soon, in a polite but cold tone. Everything considered, Amin had not made an impressive showing except for his manner of arrival, which was the first indication I had that this man was no ordinary head of state. For a moment, one could glimpse the popular aura around him that he would develop quite successfully in time, especially as he gained more confidence.

The students, meanwhile, had raised an important political issue: that exploitation bears no particular colour, that it is the defining property of a class and not of a race. It was not long before echoes of this came from beyond the grounds of the university. Amin maintained that Asian businessmen were responsible for exploitation in the market and that all would be rectified with the transfer of businesses into African hands. All, however, was not rectified. With the first transfer of business (later revoked) it became clear that an African businessman, newly established, under unstable political conditions, must of necessity charge more than his Asian predecessor. One began to hear charges that 'black Asians' had arisen within the nation. A most incredible debate on capitalist morality followed in the letters to the editor column of the Uganda Argus. What is legitimate rent? What is legitimate profit? Of course, it will take time – one hopes not too long – for this debate to be resolved.

The student rally in City Square had been followed by Amin outlawing NUSU, and paratroopers were sent onto the university. At every

© Baileys African History Archive

Sealing Asians' shops

prominent place on the campus, one could see a couple of paratroopers marching up and down, their guns displayed at their sides. One wondered what was to follow.

It was now October, the time for the guild to hold its annual election. The president of the guild for years had been from the left. The question on every student's mind was: will the left put up a candidate this year?

In the election there were three candidates. One was a Muganda, the son of a prominent landlord. To the students, he was the candidate of the establishment. The second was an ex-soldier who had become a successful businessman, and had now returned to the university. His identification was with the top of the establishment, particularly with Amin. The last candidate was from the north, the part of the country Obote had come from, a region that had sent a number of left-wing activists to the campus. The choice was clear.

Traditionally, university elections are quite lively. The campaign goes beyond campus issues like the running of the canteen or the adequacy of the dining-hall food service. It is an explicitly ideological campaign, centring on the nature of development policy within the country and particularly on the relationship of the campus with society at large.

Contrary to expectations, the left on the campus refused to sit out the elections. The campaign itself became particularly active and also rather colourful. I remember one evening strolling by the tennis courts at around six o'clock, coming up to Mary Stuart Hall, a women's hall of residence, and finding a political rally in progress. About 150 students seemed to have gathered, 30 of them holding placards. One of these read, 'Civilian Government at Makerere'. Shocked at such a bold display of political sentiment, I went a little closer. It was a left-wing rally. The group of students were surrounded by 20 or so paratroopers who were themselves surrounded by another ring of 150 to 200 students. The slogans were all explicitly anti-military government. The paratroopers looked most uneasy, unable to decide whether by their presence they were condoning the proceedings or being a check on more drastic action by the students. At a loss as to what to do, they just stood there, silent but ill at ease. The speeches were followed by jubilant rallies up and down the numerous roads on this sprawling campus.

A week later the elections were held. The voting was heavy. The results showed an overwhelming victory for the left, which received nearly 60 per cent of the votes. So the stand-off between the students and Amin, despite the paratroopers on campus, was continuing.

An event took place at about this time which effectively brought this stand-off to an end. On precisely the day the organised airlift of Asians was to begin, a ground attack was launched by guerrillas (Ugandans) from nearby Tanzania. After his overthrow in 1971 ex-president Obote had found sanctuary in nearby Tanzania with whose leader, Julius Nyerere, he shared ideological convictions as well as a personal friendship. A number of his ministers and a sizable part of the army followed Obote into Tanzania. Across the border, in Tanzania to the south and Sudan to the north, they established military training camps. The Sudan camp closed down after Amin assisted in bringing to a conclusion the civil war between the Sudanese central government and the southern Anyanya rebels. Many of the Anyanya ex-guerrillas now formed Amin's security officers, organised into a ruthless and efficient intelligence network by the Israelis. The majority of Amin's opponents, however, were in Tanzania. Perhaps calculating that Amin might be at his most vulnerable now that he was isolated from Britain and had to withstand the dislocation – social and economic – of the mass expulsion of Asians just underway, the guerrillas attacked. The effect, of course, was the opposite of what was intended.

Certainly, there had been divisions among Amin's previous supporters, ethnic splits within the army, discontent with the regime's increasingly Muslim orientation, etc. But the invasion of left-wing Obote guerrillas launched from nearby socialist Tanzania served to underline the common class interests of all the competing groups, reminding them of their common interests in supporting Amin. The invasion served to consolidate Amin's ranks, at precisely the time he needed it most, as no other event could have done. Tactically, it had been a monumental blunder. It also gave Amin precisely the opportunity he needed to crack down on all serious internal opposition, that is all class opposition to the nascent African bourgeoisie. The axe came down on the different groups. First it came down on all known left-wing activists and sympathisers, from John Kakonge and Basil Bataringaya (both active in the left wing of Obote's Uganda People's Congress), and from Frank Kalimuzo (the university vice-chancellor, a known Obote supporter) to well-known student socialists (Kisimbo Masiko, the president of the NUSU and Tumusiime Mutebile, the president of the guild). The second group it came down on was the leading Catholics in the country: Benedicto Kiwanuka (then the chief justice and previously the head of the Democratic Party), Father Kiggunda (editor of the Catholic paper, *Munno*), Joseph Mabiru (a former president of the Bank of Uganda and now working for the Asian industrialist Madhvani) and Nekenia Bananuka (the paramount chief of the Ankole people).

The emphasis on Catholicism was only apparently a religious one; it fact its substance was political. Ever since the 1900 agreement through which the British lavishly gave miles of land to Baganda Protestant chiefs, the Catholic hierarchy had been in opposition, sometimes even articulating the grievances of the oppressed tenant peasantry. In the 1950s, when the Kabaka of Buganda and his parliament, the Lukiko (an organ of the Protestant landlords) fought for the secession of Buganda from Uganda and boycotted the national elections, the Baganda Catholics organised the Democratic Party (DP) to participate in these same elections. Their newspaper was *Munno*. The Protestant hierarchy dubbed the DP as Dini Ya Pap (in Swahili, the religion of the Pope). Internally, Amin's coup represented an alliance of a law and order army, a typically large and pampered colonial bureaucracy whose privileges Obote had begun to curtail, the Baganda landed oligarchy and the small Baganda bourgeoisie (primarily Muslim and Protestant) against an increasingly left-leaning

Obote government with its Common Man's Charter and its corresponding nationalisation of business.

During the 90 days, the Western press began to speak of the sophisticated, intellectual Baganda becoming disillusioned with the son of the soil, Amin. But Amin's crackdown had not been on the Baganda but on Baganda Catholics. The Baganda establishment, the Protestant establishment, cheered – but as we shall see, not for too long.

On the campus, Amin had banned NUSU. Plainclothes men began attending lectures. There were rumours that the government believed leading members of the student left had been in contact with the guerrillas and had in fact organised an underground movement. Army presence on the campus was reinforced. One evening the television announcer read a list of names of people who had 'decided to disappear'. It included the vice-chancellor of the university, a particularly popular figure among the students. The next day the army came and took him away.

A number of the guerrillas were said to have come from the western region, particularly Kigezi. Kigezi was a region where, in the 1940s, the cooperative movement spread far and wide among the farming community. Unlike other areas, the movement in Kigezi was particularly politicised and democratic. In the late 1950s the left wing of the movement organised various discussion groups in the rural high schools. There they spoke of colonial rule, of the resources of the country and of who controlled them and who produced them. The students who came out of these high schools and went on to the university provided political leadership on the campus, beginning in the late 1960s. It was these students who were suspected by the government of having organised a left-wing underground. The aim of Amin's policy was to isolate them.

It was now clear that Amin was no longer willing to sit and see the campus turn into a centre of opposition to his government. With the arrest of the vice-chancellor, the stakes of opposition were getting higher. The number of people willing to put themselves at risk were fewer. In the midst of this came a week of celebrations for the university's jubilee. Ceremonial trees, arches, flags and banners went up as previously planned. The programme, however, was cut to a minimum. Nevertheless, there was a programme, pipes at noon and traditional dancing in the evening, along with guards everywhere. It all seemed bizarre and surreal. The vice-chancellor was in custody, perhaps dead. On Convocation Day the chancellor – Amin himself – was to address the students, the staff and guests. Four days prior to the convocation, it was announced that Amin wished to address the students on the next day. All must be present.

'Why does the man have to come here three days before he is going to be here anyway?' The question was asked over and over again. Fear and apprehension were written on every face. The military presence was once again reinforced on the day of Amin's arrival. Students gathered in the main hall and the gathering overflowed into the surrounding grounds, which had been wired with loud speakers. It was hot.

As usual, Amin was late. My fingers twitched nervously, wondering how many would share the fate of the vice-chancellor. When he came his first comment was that it was particularly stuffy in the theatre; shouldn't everybody go outside onto the grounds, where the jubilee celebrations would be held anyway? Outside, there was a little breeze and one could stretch. Amin stood there, laughing, jovial, obviously attempting to put everybody at ease, behaving like a grandfather, yet presiding over an event that, with the accentuated presence of the military, had wrecked everybody's nerves. Lest some fuzzy-headed academic might get the wrong idea, Amin had made certain, by having the army there, that it would be clear to all present who had the power and who could call the tune. Now he seemed so jovial, that all relaxed a little. Surely he wouldn't be laughing like this if he wanted to put us all in gaol?

Unlike the time I had heard him before at City Square, he wisely decided not to read from a prepared text. Instead, he spoke impromptu and was both coherent and witty. It was clear that he had not come there to say anything specific. His purpose was to let the students know he was very much around, to get them to forget what had happened on campus, particularly the disappearance of the vice-chancellor, and to make them feel at ease with him. These objectives could only be achieved by a certain kind of performance, not by the substance of a speech. He succeeded remarkably well.

As I sat there I felt terribly antagonistic to the man. Then seeing this crowd of people turn from tense silence to nervous giggles and finally to completely abandoned laughter, I felt antagonistic to the audience as well. Somewhere along the way I started listening to Amin. I realised the man was a masterful performer. He had in fact succeeded in isolating the left from the rest of the student body. In between all the jokes and stories there was a clear message: if they sat quiet and consented, all would be well; if not, they would follow the vice-chancellor.

In the coming weeks I had more opportunities to hear Amin, more importantly, to witness him act with the decisiveness of a tiger. As the weeks went by, every Sunday brought us further analysis from the Western press. Amin was a madman, he was uneducated, and he was a religious zealot. Together, these personal attributes were supposed to explain his actions. To me this all sounded ludicrous.

Amin may be formally uneducated (he has only a primary four education). In real terms, however, he is very well educated. He is a man who has an accurate understanding of his own social environment, a clear grasp of his goals and a very good tactical sense of how to achieve them. He is thus able to embark on a realistic strategy to attain his objectives. Even when he invokes divine inspiration and support, as he has done to justify every one of his actions, Amin is being more astute. He has displayed a remarkable understanding of the importance of ideology in creating legitimacy. For the urban classes he has nationalism and militarism, for the peasantry he prescribes religion. Those who ridicule him or deride him as being uneducated really judge him in the abstract, outside of his own social context. As his opponents learned so dearly, it is as much of a mistake to underestimate this man as it is to glorify him.

When he claimed overwhelming support for the economic war, the expulsion of Asians, Amin was not indulging in idle boast. The politically conscious classes, with the exception of some students of peasant background, supported him totally.

To appreciate Amin's strength, however, is not to condone his politics. In fact, I had little sympathy with this man and his attempt to create a semi-fascist state. 'Fascist' because the object of his policies is to organise all of society's resources, human and material, and put them at the service of capital, African capital. (This is why the road to fascism may take him through a number of progressive steps, for it may mean an assault on international capital.) And 'semi' because Uganda's productive resources are not sufficiently advanced to permit him the sort of organisation and control that was possible for fascist Japan.

It was because of the class content of his policies that the invasion from leftist Tanzania served to consolidate power. It made certain that as long as the economic war continued, Amin would enjoy undivided support, regardless of his ethnic and religious excesses. For Amin was doing the dirty work. This is why it is also conceivable that once this dirty work was over, once the old society had given way to the new, the social issues had been dealt with and the technical issues had come to the fore, Amin might cease to be useful and be cast aside. For the moment, at least, his iron will, his clarity of purpose and his popular approach seemed indispensable, especially since the class in whose interest he was acting, the tiny African bourgeoisie, lacked all of these.

5 DEPARTURE: LOOKING TOWARDS BRITAIN

DESPITE THE physical harassment and even killings in the countryside, the exodus began with but a trickle. For the first month and a half the refugee flights to Britain went half-empty. Even the few who had been issued entry permits by the British felt reluctant to leave immediately. The high commission itself had encountered the feeling that the Uganda government might be persuaded to exempt more categories of people, and that at least the deadline might be extended from the original three months to perhaps a year.

Those who tried to leave were systematically robbed by rank and file soldiers on the way to the airport. The Uganda government, realising that theft was perhaps *the* factor delaying the departure of many Asians, arranged for armed police to escort buses to the airport. With the high commission more cooperative, and the Ugandan government anxious to expedite the expulsion process, a larger stream of Asians began to leave.

During the last few weeks in Uganda our thoughts wandered to Britain. What would it be like there? Every colonial child grew up with the notion that the motherland was the greenest pasture on earth, that the English tree had the sweetest fruit. In those last few weeks in Uganda there began a daily countdown on the television and radio. 'The British Asians should realise that they have only 14 days to leave for their homeland, Britain.' England now seemed far more imminent.

The immediate experiences of England were those with the English officialdom in Uganda. Certainly the experience with the British high commission had not been a pleasant one. The 1968 Commonwealth Immigration Act and the quota voucher system for non-white British subjects had called forth numerous bitter demonstrations on the part of the worst hit of the Asian British citizens in Uganda. Even after Amin's expulsion order, the high commission had been reluctant to budge from the quota system. The reports in the British press gave the impression of a public panic. To us it seemed as if the hysteria had been generated, at least in part, by the government itself. They seemed to be getting ready for us as one prepares for a swarm of locusts.

When the high commission rented another building to cope with the long queues and additional staff was brought over from England, they naturally called for people who had had some experience in dealing with Uganda Asians. What this meant in practice was that the reinforcements primarily comprised of immigration officials who had worked at the London airports, keeping an eye on any Asians who might be trying to slip through the immigration net. Their view of the world was particularly conspiratorial. To them, as we had ample opportunities to witness, every affidavit was false, every statement was a lie and every Asian was an inscrutable oriental whose intentions had to be scrutinised most carefully.

In October the *Daily Nation*, a Nairobi paper, sent a reporter to England to give an eyewitness account of the reception of the new immigrants. His report was hardly encouraging. He visited London and Leicester and wrote extensively of the graffiti on the tube station walls, on posters, on buildings, everywhere: 'wogs out.' To top it all, the Uganda Argus carried a series of advertisements from the city of Leicester. The message was clear: there are too many Asians here already, so please go elsewhere. The advertisement, however, backfired. Most people by then had heard of England and of London. But now they knew there was some place called Leicester, where there were numerous Asians. All those who had been undecided as to where to go, and there were many, after reading of the hostile reactions of the British public in general, started making arrangements to go to Leicester.

Every day busloads of people departed for the airport. In the confusion, there was never time to see more than a few people before departure. For those who were staying behind, it became a daily ritual to go to Airways House in the evening and say goodbye to any familiar faces there. This was, however, not a usual goodbye, for everybody would be leaving sooner or later. Yet, in most cases, there were no addresses to be exchanged. One wondered if one would ever see the friend again. After each bus had left there was the same gloom, the same feeling of hopelessness and despair. Soon we stopped going to Airways House. By the first week of November, my family, my relations and my Asian friends had left. I had stayed behind to finish my work at the university, to correct student essays and examinations and to turn in marks.

AN IMPORTANT ANNOUNCEMENT ON BEHALF OF THE COUNCIL OF THE CITY OF LEICESTER, ENGLAND

The City council of Leicester, England, believe that many families in Uganda are considering moving to Leicester.

If YOU are thinking of doing so, it is very important you should know that PRESENT CONDITIONS IN THE CITY ARE VERY DIFFERENT FROM THOSE MET BY EARLIER SETTLERS. They are: –

HOUSING – several thousands of families are already on the Council's waiting list

EDUCATION – hundreds of children are awaiting places in the schools

SOCIAL AND HEALTH SERVICES – already stretched to the limit

IN YOUR OWN INTERESTS AND THOSE OF YOUR FAMILY YOU SHOULD ACCEPT THE ADVICE OF THE UGANDA RESETTLEMENT BOARD AND NOT COME TO LEICESTER

The text of an advertisement placed in Uganda newspapers by Leicester City Council

The last week at home had been particularly difficult. Every night my parents and I went to sleep to the sound of gunfire. On the Tuesday of the last week in October a nasty rumour had floated through Kampala that Amin had ordered the arbitrary arrest and death of over a hundred Asian families. Nobody stopped to question the truth of this, though we endlessly discussed the reasons behind it. To be prudent then meant to believe the worst, or so it seemed. The next day we left our home and separated out into safer parts of the city. I went to the University guesthouse. In a few days my parents left. The following day I went back home with a number of American and British friends. Would they please take whatever they wanted? Television, cushions, sheets, pots and pans, flowerpots, furniture, yes, everything. This had been a home with most of its contents having been accumulated over time. Now it had come down like a house of cards. The belongings were not just any flowerpots, records, cushions, but rather my mother's flowerpots, brother's records, sister's cushions. Before leaving the house I looked out from the balcony. In the distance I could see tiny mud huts, their tin roofs glistening under the hot tropical sun, each the home of a family. I wondered what difference our expulsion would make to their future.

A few days later I left. My English and American friends came to Airways House to see me off. In those days, for an African to be seen with an Asian was a risk to both lives. It was sufficient evidence of intended sabotage. Even two months earlier, when I had gone to see Maria, a friend at the university, she had pleaded, 'Please Mahmood, we can't go out together. Don't you know how things have changed? It's not me, it's the times. I'm sorry.'

As I boarded the bus for the airport and looked out of the window to wave goodbye, John made one last attempt to make light of the situation.

'Make sure this is the last time you are kicked out of a country on charges of being a bourgeois!'

Uganda Asians walking to board their plane at Entebbe airport, 1972

I tried hard to laugh. But I felt as if someone dear to me had died. At the airport, there was the expected long queue and the endless arguments about whether the weight of one's baggage was excessive. Once into the lounge, the old collapsed into the cushioned chairs, the babies went to sleep, and the young took to some serious drinking. While emptying my second glass of Uganda Waragi (a drink with a banana base), I felt a hand firmly grip my shoulder. It was Ahmed, an old high school friend; his brother was a major in the army. The last I had seen of him was early in September when we had bitterly argued over the political implications of Amin's decree and the class basis of his support. He ordered two drinks. Without saying a word, we gulped them down. I tried to reciprocate the gesture. He held my hand and ordered a second round and then a third. The loudspeakers announced it was time to embark. I got up and arranged my hand luggage. Ahmed extended his hand.

'Goodbye comrade.' 'Goodbye brother.'

Once on the East African Airways plane I took my seat and tried to sleep, but sleep I could not.

'A drink,' the ever-smiling and polite hostess suggested.

'No, thank you.' I had drugged myself with enough drink already. I tried to look out the window. It was too dark. Just as well. But I could still see clearly in my mind my home, or rather, the different houses we had lived in while my father moved up from petty clerk to a well-to-do auctioneer, in times when commerce had been lucrative, when an hour of a trader's labour was worth days of a labourer's work. I could see the mosque around which we played as children, the primary school that we used to walk to early in the morning, carrying our lunch packages of chapatti and curried potatoes; the years in secondary school when, as a boy scout, I went climbing the mountains, trekking through the swamps and savannas of the countryside, swimming in ponds and lakes and learning to climb trees the way a monkey does; and the day I heard I was one of the 23 sponsored by the Uganda government for further studies in the United States, the day every mother hopes for but fears (for in colonial parlance, education could only be overseas).

Later, there came a political awakening in the United States, the civil rights marches in the south and the Vietnam rallies. Tragedy, then, was always something that happened to other people. Finally, after just summer holidays in Uganda, I had come back home, home to my parents, home to friends and home to the land. The thrill as I began teaching at the university had suddenly melted as the last 90 days began. In the midst of people who had spent their entire lives in the country and who were about to lose everything they had ever had or known, it seemed selfish to feel sorry for myself. But the 90 days had not been just a tragic event; they taught me a political lesson, a very simple lesson, but a lesson I would learn again in my next 90 days in Britain: unless you belong to the class that rules, a good argument will never be enough to safeguard your interests. Unless you are willing to sacrifice some of your immediate interests, and thus form a community with others, your future can never be secured.

The long journey had suddenly come to an end. The captain was announcing that the weather over London was 'overcast.'

PART TWO

6 Arrival

'ARE YOU sure it is 10 in the morning? It looks more like 6 in the evening.'
'Oh yes, it is 10. Just you wait. You'll soon learn to talk about the weather first thing in the morning.'

We had disembarked at Heathrow. Having passed through London some years ago as a student, I thought I would share my experience of English weather with my fellow passengers. We walked up a long hallway, clean, almost clinical, like a stretched-out hospital corridor.

'Your vaccination certification please.' Queuing had by now become a reflex action with us. So we queued as we tried to hold onto our pieces of luggage and fumble through our papers to get to our health certificates.

With the health formalities over, another corridor lead us into the main immigration room. There were three queues: British, Commonwealth and Irish, and All Other Nationals. I confidently walked over to the official on the British desk and handed him my passport.

'Sorry, you must queue in the Commonwealth section.'

'But we are British.'

'Yes, I know.'

'So things still haven't changed,' I hissed under my breath. Asians with British passports had had to join the Commonwealth queue before, and apparently now as well. But, as it turned out, the Uganda Resettlement Board had its people at the Commonwealth section, eight of them, an Indian, an American, two Canadians and the rest English. The English volunteers, except one, were all women. This would become an established pattern in the camps. The volunteers were always women. English men inevitably represented officialdom.

We sat around waiting to be individually cleared. Three older women, wearing what looked like green girl-guide uniforms, took turns serving coffee with tea or biscuits. For children, there was orange drink. The processing took little time. My turn came around quickly.

'Yes, young man, do you know anyone in England?'

'Yes, my parents are in a camp. Could I please join them?' 'Let me see ... Yes ... it's Kensington Student Centre. They have no doctor there. Would you please step aside so we can x-ray you?'

Another ten minutes and the x-ray was over. Clearly, the staff here were experienced and efficient. In the meantime, an older Asian lady had joined me. She was also to be taken to Kensington, but her luggage had been misplaced. She spoke but a few words of English.

'Please don't leave me. I know I am old and slow, and a burden on a young man like you. But please, stay with me until we get to the camp.'

'Certainly,' I said. But she was not convinced. Every few minutes, while we looked for and finally found her luggage, she kept on repeating the same request; each time, it sounded more like a desperate plea. I was very tired, and gradually sympathy gave way to irritation.

What we expected to be a few minutes' interruption in this efficient process was turning out to be a tedious four-hour wait, while they decided on a mode of transport for us. I talked to the lady for a while and then tried to read a little. The volunteers stood in a corner talking to each other; we sat in another corner keeping to ourselves. The Indian volunteer must have realised that we were both tired and restless; he crossed over and tried to talk a little of Uganda.

'You want to go to Kensington? Would you please follow me?' I realised that English volunteer was talking to me. 'We'll take a taxi,' he said. Great, soon I'll be in the camp! Between the two of us there were three suitcases, four handbags and a sitar.

'Anything to declare?' the customs official stopped us. The volunteer gave me an inquiring look. Surely, there must have been a mistake, I thought.

'We have just come from Uganda and brought along whatever we could of our possessions. Surely, you are not going to charge us customs duty?'

'I am afraid you must declare goods like anybody else coming into this country. And if there is a customs duty to be paid, you must pay it.'

'But isn't there any exemption for Asians from Uganda?'

'No, sir, I am sorry. Nobody is entitled to special treatment.'

Special treatment? Don't special circumstances *demand* special treatment? I felt I was entering an alien world. Carefully, the official went through our luggage. Fortunately, there was nothing that should have been declared.

Once outside, the volunteer looked for a taxi.

'I'm sorry, there seems to be no taxi. Shall we take a bus?' Was he asking my opinion, or politely informing me of the next course of action? It was the latter.

We got into the bus, and then into another, switching to the underground and finally to a third bus. Every time I got on or off the bus I managed to bang my sitar against a railing. I wondered if I had cracked it. 'Oh, what did it matter,' I thought.

The volunteer was a man of few words. With not even a hello, the conversation was kept down to a few instructional sentences that he uttered at the end or beginning of every ride. I realised he was becoming somewhat uneasy and embarrassed as numerous passengers gave us hostile, or certainly unfriendly, glances. A little boy asked his mother:

'Mother, who are they?'

'They are refugees, darling.'

'What's he carrying, Mother?'

"It's an *Indian* instrument, darling. Now why don't you be quiet, dear?'

Finally, we got off the bus and walked into the camp, a large sturdy brick structure. Another volunteer took over.

'Ah, yes. You go to Room 44. And get your linen along the way. Just a minute, I'll show you where to get it.'

Room 44 seemed to be 30 feet by 10 feet with eight beds arranged in hospital fashion. Four beds were already occupied, and the fifth was mine. Gradually the four occupants came in, one after another. They had all arrived either just a few hours or days before me. For the next two and a half months we would live together in the same room.

The first to greet me was Patel, in his late 30s, married, with three children. He said he had sent his wife and children to India, hoping to call them to England once he had settled down and found himself a house and a job. Patel spoke very little English. In Gujarati, however, he was a man of many words.

'What will you do?'

'I am willing to do anything. I am a hard worker you know. In Uganda, 20 years ago, I tried to go into trade up-country, but I had no money. That was the time of the 1950 trade boycott, and nobody would give me a long-term loan. So I would come to Kampala, buy things on loan – candles, *maricani* cloth, torches, knives, pencils, anything – and take them up-country by bus and sell them to small peddlers. My brothers were better off. But nobody thought I could succeed. The last few years, I used to work 13 to 15 hours a day, collapsing every six months or so. Even the doctor said I should take a rest. But no, not V.B. Patel. You know, last year I bought a car. Of course, it was secondhand. But it helped me a lot. I could make more deliveries and make them at any time I chose to. And then Amin Dada signed this decree and I was back to zero. But I didn't stop working. I didn't spend my money. Did I know whether Amin would change his mind? No, I wasn't going to take any chances. But that is all in the past. We're all here now, brother, all of us at zero,' he laughed.

'Don't you listen to him. He says he works hard. But all he does here is sleep,' someone else chided.

It was true, and I noticed as the days went by that Patel was beginning to spend more of his day, not to mention night, in bed. Once I prodded him about this. He just smiled and said, 'Oh, I am becoming lazy.' But I persisted.

'What do you expect? I am not educated like you. To speak to anyone important here, one has to speak English. To leave this camp, one has to speak English. The only thing I can do without speaking English is sleep.'

For a man who had worked so hard in his previous environment, Patel was becoming increasingly lazy. But laziness was not a natural trait; it was a response to a particular set of social circumstances. The circumstances of the camp, where knowledge of English was a prerequisite to gaining access to any facility, were hardly suited to encouraging the industrious side of Patel's personality.

When we first went out to the pub, Patel refused to come. Later, when he did come, he was extremely nervous. He watched every movement of the people around him, and copied them to the minutest detail. It seemed he was in mortal fear of doing something wrong. He spoke to an English person only when spoken to, and then he always addressed the person as 'Sir' or 'Madam,' continuously apologising for his broken English. Never could he forget that this was England – the other world, the better world, the white man's world – and that he was Indian, worse still, a dark Indian who could not speak fluent English. One day, when he had ventured to go out on a walk by himself, he came back and asked me: 'What is a wog, Mahmood?'

In the corner slept Benjamin Desa, a Goan in his early 30s, slightly overweight, with a receding hairline, features he became most conscious of over time. A bachelor, he had been a teacher in Uganda. He had always wanted to come to England, but on his fixed income and carefree existence, there were never sufficient savings for foreign travel. From the day I met him, he was anxious to take a walk. Later he admitted he thought there would be lots of women in the streets, particularly friendly women. He went out a couple of times, saying hello to a number of women who looked nice. The response, if one could call it that, was a cold stare. He returned rather puzzled.

'Perhaps it is my weight and hair, or the lack of it.' He tried to make light of it, but then added, 'We must find out where we can meet Indian women.'

For those who came from the colonies, there was a very mixed pre-conception of the mother country. England was regarded with awe. One expected to be dazzled by its beauty, its wealth and its splendour. Surely, London will have the most majestic of all buildings, the widest of all wide streets, and even the longest of all possible traffic jams. English beer will be the most intoxicating of all brews, chugged down the most delicate of all gullets. And English women – yes – what with their legendary beauty, charm and availability. To the colonial child, England was the rainbow on the horizon.

But the English were also the colonial masters, the oppressors, the others. One's only knowledge of the English was founded on colonial experiences. Having experienced discrimination in Uganda, one expected it in England.

How many times, when in the midst of an unpleasant situation, did I ask myself the question: am I making this all up or is this for real?

History was catching up with England. The colonial child had come to the motherland. And he had brought with him England's colonial past. Past had become present.

Next to me was Singh. Always laughing and joking, SS, as he was called, breathed life into the room. He had been an architect's assistant in Uganda and he was just staying in the room for a week or so, 'until they have made arrangements for me to leave for Argentina'.

'But why do you want to go to Argentina?'

'They say it's nice and warm there. Here, I'm always hidden under clothing, and my body lost in the midst of all this concrete and metal,' he said as his arms made a wide and expansive gesture that seemed to take in the entire city around us. But then he turned and added, with a deci-siveness in his voice that suggested he was finally making his point: 'Look, in Kampala I worked for a British firm. I know how it is. If you have this colour,' he said, rubbing his forefinger against the skin on his hand, 'your place in the hierarchy is fixed. In Argentina, at least my chances would depend on my abilities and nothing else.' For better or for worse, it took two months, and not two weeks, for the formalities to be completed. By then SS had made a number of friends in the camp and some outside. He had even found a job. Like everyone else, he was haunted by the spectre of loneliness; he decided not to go to Argentina.

Kaka, in his late 50s, was the oldest of us all. His wife and children were in India. 'Why doesn't he go to India?' One could read this question on the face of most camp officials when they met Kaka. I had become accustomed to the question though, for it was asked by all hostile Britons and plagued a number of sympathetic ones too: 'Why don't these Asians, whether they hold British passports or not, go to India? Why, after all, this clamour to get into Britain?'

In fact, a number of Uganda Asians had gone to India. But these were only the people who had either considerable assets or prosperous relatives in India. The vast majority who went to Britain (or Canada) faced one inescapable fact: the bottom of the economic ladder in England was far preferable to that in India. The very reason why the British had ventured out to Africa and Asia in an earlier era, and why individual Britons still emigrate overseas – the search for a better material life – was behind the Asians' desire to come to Britain. It was reflected in Kaka, who wanted to find a job, 'any job, in a factory, anywhere, work for two years, save some money, and go back to India.'

In those days, every one of us had quite specific plans, with details of what we wanted to do, but little idea of how we would set about doing it.

That first evening, after dinner, we ventured to the camp gate, which opened onto Kensington Church Street. It was about 9 in the evening, and we stood there looking at the people passing by. One group, two couples and an older lady, stopped and asked if we were Uganda Asians.

'*Uganda* Asians? Of course, yes we are.' It struck me that in the past three months in Uganda we had been collectively referred to as the British Asians; now in Britain, we would be called Uganda Asians. They started talking, were slightly tipsy, but very nice. One of them was paraphrasing the rather mixed welcome message *The Economist* had put on its cover the month before.

'We know we didn't always want you here, and we know you didn't really want to come, but now that you are here, we are glad. Let's learn to live together.'

'But we *did* want to come,' one of the group broke in.

The conversation shifted to Amin.

'He's really a Julius Caesar, isn't he?'

'Yes, it's a shame there is no Brutus.'

The older woman looked up, a little startled.

'My, they are civilised, aren't they? Listen to the English they speak.'

'If we were in France, they wouldn't think we were civilised because we spoke good English.'

That stopped things a little. We all realised there was no need for bitterness, so the topic was changed. We talked amiably for another ten minutes and then went our separate ways.

The next morning, after breakfast, we were back at the gate. On the other side of the street a number of people stood in a bus queue, most of them reading a morning paper.

'Something important has happened, perhaps in Uganda. Let's go get a paper,' somebody suggested. Gradually, sometimes amusingly, but not always so, we were learning of English habits. That evening we ventured out of the gate again, this time going a bit further down Church Street and along the busy-looking street at the corner. It was Kensington High Street: Barker's, Derry and Toms, Woolworths...

'This is like 20 Draper's (the largest clothing store in Kampala) put into one,' Ben remarked, as he peered into Derry and Toms.

'Yes, it's like all of Kampala put into one street,' SS agreed. We had read of the English as being a nation of shopkeepers.

This seemed more like a nation of shoppers. We walked around, gradually, looking at window displays, reading advertisements, translating pounds into Uganda shillings, generally absorbed by all the things around us. The people were rushing by too quickly to be examined individually. At the tube station, however, there were two long queues, one in front of the bus stop, another at the newspaper stand.

'Look at the women. Incredible!' Yes, they were quite incredible or, rather, strange. Like a parade of exotic creatures in a national game park: every shade of cosmetic one could have imagined, hair from jet black to colourless stringy blonde, their faces set with definite expressions – life on stage.

'Look at her, she must have been a zebra in her previous life.' 'But look behind her, that's definitely a gazelle.'

The gazelle represented a different breed, definitely a minority, not

Barker's and Derry and Toms department stores on Kensington High Street
in the early 1970s

so obviously made up, very much the product of what must have been a
most delicate and complex process, sans colour, sans taste, sans odour;
ethereal, like air.

'It must be hard work to be a woman in this place. I don't think I
would like it.' Patel summed up our feelings.

In the next few days, however, we realised that it wasn't such a nice
feeling to walk up and down Kensington High Street among people who
seemed to be buying things just about all the time. Our resources were
limited to social security payments of £2.10 a week. With such a meagre
income, buying anything was out of the question. But all around us was
incessant consumption; staring at us from every window were things just

waiting to be bought, to be eaten, to be worn, to be read. Large and small signs, they all urged one to acquire and made one feel deprived, however temporary the feeling might be.

One of the signs read: 'Don't you need a new coat this winter?' Of course, we needed it. But our demand was not what the economist calls 'effective demand'. In the market place, where the demand curve meets the supply curve, we had no resources to represent our needs. Under such circumstances, looking at life on Kensington High Street seemed like seeing the city through its ass-hole.

Gradually, we began to acquire habits that people usually associated with the lower classes – in Uganda, with the African domestic servants. Every Friday, we received our £2.10 social security. By Sunday, it was all gone, on cigarettes and drinks. All the money, however, was very little money. It didn't take many weeks to realise that saving makes sense only to those whose incomes are above a certain level. To those who have very little to begin with, there is little incentive to save. One's position in the social hierarchy, and its vast influence on the shaping of individual or group life, was gradually becoming clear to us.

7   THE CAMP I

'YOU'RE COLD. Why don't you go downstairs and get a warm sweater and a coat? It's free. There's a women's voluntary organisation that hands it out. Come, I'll show you where it is.' Ben led me downstairs, to the WRVS clothing room.

'You are...?'

'Mamdani.'

'OK, Mr Mamdani. I have got a coat just for you. It's a Parisian cape. Only slightly worn. Not more than two years old. And a hat to go with it. My, it's from Harrods too.' She examined the hat, and then added, 'Harrods – that's where the rich in this country do their shopping.'

Fitted in my Parisian cape and a Harrods' bowler hat, with wire-rimmed glasses, a bushy moustache, and curly black hair coming out from under the black hat, I must have looked quite ridiculous. As I strolled out into the car park that fills the space between the two large concrete buildings that were the camp, the young Nigerian car attendant looked me up and down:

'Hey man, what you need is an umbrella.' He broke out into peals of laughter.

Standing next to me was a smartly dressed middle-aged lady, waiting to pay her parking fee. Trying hard to conceal the smile on her face, she turned to her dog, a well-groomed white poodle that she led by a chain. I followed her gaze. Heavens, even the dog was clothed! There seemed a curious similarity between the poodle and me: both dressed in the ways of an alien world. For a few seconds, the car attendant and the lady seemed to share this realisation – and they laughed freely. The next moment, however, the lady seemed embarrassed and apologetic; she hurried through the ticket payment and hastily walked to her car. The Nigerian just shook his head.

'The Man's got you, boy.' I wondered whatever he meant, if anything at all.

What I couldn't miss was the fact that there was something wrong with the cape–hat–Asian combination. Once back in the room, I discarded the bowler hat. It was time for my morning visit to my parents.

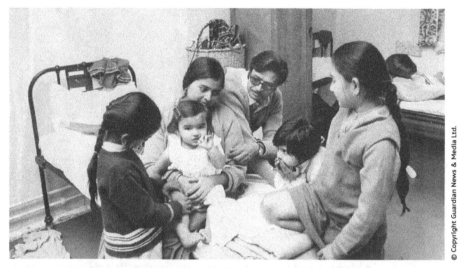

© Copyright Guardian News & Media Ltd.

Mr Jagdesh Jani with his wife and four children in the
Kensington Student Centre camp, 11 September 1972

Unlike most other couples, who shared rooms with single and other
married people, my parents had a room all to themselves; two beds fitted
into a six by eight box-room. I met my father in the corridor. Mother had
been sick the night before, with vomiting, fever and fainting spells. Would
I take her downstairs to the Red Cross? At the Red Cross – a storeroom
converted into an emergency health centre – there was a line of eight
people, most of them down with flu. It meant a 45-minute wait.

'You have a slight fever. Look, why don't you take some codeine
water? Four times a day. It will also help you sleep.'

That night, however, the vomiting increased and the fever would not
subside. The next day, the lady at the Red Cross arranged an appointment
with a local doctor.

'Take her in a taxi. I'll reimburse you.'

Partly dazed, mostly ill with fever, Mother could hardly walk.

I helped her into a taxi, and to the doctor's.

'She's in a terrible shape. Could she please see the doctor immediately?'

'Yes, but first her name and address.'

The doctor looked an amiable person, immaculately dressed.

His office seemed more like a lawyer's library. 'She has been here
before, hasn't she?'

'No she hasn't.'

'And you're quite sure?'

'Yes, quite.'

'Well, they all look the same, don't they?'

I gritted my teeth, blood flowing to my eyes. I tried to look at my mother, and think of her illness, and forget about this doctor.

Back at the camp, I walked up to the canteen. A meeting was in progress, addressed by the camp administrator and his assistant, Mrs Maxwell.

'I don't want to see anybody but camp residents eat here. If you have any friends or relations from Leicester or Southall coming to visit you, you must come to me before you take them into the dining room with you. For each guest, you'll have to pay 25p. And remember, only I can grant permission.'

'Under what circumstances would you refuse permission?' I asked.

'Do you live here?'

'Yes.'

'Well, that's for you to find out.'

The meeting moved onto the next point on the agenda: the menu. There had been complaints about the monotony of the diet.

'This is not your home. It's a refugee camp, remember. You can't expect everything here.'

'Sir, it's not that the diet is monotonous, it's deficient. You can see the lines of people at the Red Cross every morning. All we eat is starch: rice, wheat, flour and potatoes.'

'Yes, but remember it's you people who want to cook your own vegetarian food. The non-vegetarian kitchen has no such problems.'

'True. But, don't you think you should ask a dietician to look at the menu, and then, if need be, add things like cheese, eggs and greens?'

'Hindus won't eat eggs.'

'Not all. Many vegetarians will. The others will eat greens and cheese.'

At this point, Mrs Maxwell came to the rescue: 'What we need is a catering committee. Mr Mamdani, since you are so concerned, why don't you join it?'

'Certainly, I'd be delighted.'

'And yes, that reminds me, we also need a welfare committee to deal with the problem of cleanliness. In fact, it should meet tomorrow. And there should be a catering committee person on it. Mr Mamdani, could you be that person?'

'Yes.'

The next morning, at 10am, the welfare committee met. Mrs Maxwell took the lead.

'Now, cleanliness is a primary problem. The toilets need to be watched everyday. Children are sometimes very careless. Many adults, used to Asian toilets [where the toilet bowl is in the ground and the person squats over it] are finding it difficult to use European toilets. People can take turns keeping watch. The rooms are not always clean. There must be inspection every once in a while. No socks on the floor or on the radiator. Clothing should be in suitcases or cupboards, where these are provided. Beds should be made and floors swept. We'll need a voluntary committee for this, to keep watch and inspect. The welfare committee can't do everything. Every room must have a representative who is responsible for its cleanliness.'

Quite incredible, I thought; the response to every 'problem' is another committee! Pretty soon, we will have another problem: too many committees.

'But surely, Mrs Maxwell, you don't want to turn this place into a boy scout camp, with guards and inspections all over the place,' I interrupted.

'No, not quite like that. But we need some order. Otherwise the situation will deteriorate.'

After some more discussions on how and when these committees were to be elected, the meeting focused on catering.

'Mr Mamdani, you're the catering representative. Do you wish to say anything?'

'Yes, I have decided to call a meeting of those who eat in the vegetarian kitchen this evening. We can have a thorough discussion on the menu, and on cooking and cleaning responsibilities.'

'Have you checked with the camp administrator?'

'No.'

'Well, I suggest you get his permission first.'

'His permission? Just because we are going to meet and talk about food? I see no reason for that.'

'I strongly suggest you do that. If you insist on making trouble he could take action against you.'

'Action? Like what?'

'He could throw you out of the camp.'

'OK, I'll talk to him.'

The next afternoon the catering committee met with the camp

administrator. I had been elected 'Chief Catering Officer'.

'So, Mr Mamdani, you want every person in this camp to have milk, *besides* drinking it with their tea and coffee?'

'Yes.'

'How can I sufficiently impress upon you, Mr Mamdani, that milk in liberal quantity is drunk only by a small minority of wealthy people in this country. This is not East Africa. Perhaps you should go to Leicester and Southall and see what people drink down there.'

'Well then, you must have a substitute for milk. Surely you realise that for most of us, this is our first winter. We need a healthy diet. Already a quarter of the camp has succumbed to flu.' The next week, the health visitor came. Sure enough, he found the vegetarian diet deficient. His recommendation was that it be daily supplemented with a pint of milk for children, and a half pint for adults, two ounces of cheese, dry or tinned fruit, and greens for everyone.

To the outsider, the vital issues of the camp would seem petty. The most important were: Is anyone using more blankets than they are entitled to? Did anybody consume more milk than they were entitled to? Why did Mr Patel take food into his room? Does Mr Desa have the doctor's permission to eat in his room?

In the camp there was no personal life, and this was not just because of the technical limitations of space. Far more important was the *way* the camp was run. The dictum that an administrator must gain the greatest familiarity with those who live and work under him had been closely and faithfully followed by the camp authorities. It was, however, the familiarity the master has with the affairs of the servant, not the familiarity a member of a family has with another. The contacts between the officials and the residents were thus limited to formal ones. But for these, the separation between the staff and the residents was complete.

An event which highlighted this separation was New Year's Eve. The canteen at the camp had two rooms. For two days prior to New Year's Eve, one of them was decorated rather colourfully. On the final day, a record player with loudspeakers was installed. The New Year's Eve party, however, was exclusively for the staff of the student centre and the camp administrators. Music blared while wine and champagne flowed. Guests came and went in flowing gowns and formal attire. In the next room were the camp residents, some watching television, others playing darts and the rest writing letters. For us, it was just another evening.

The only exception to administrative exclusiveness were the volunteers, two women: one American and the other English, both students. As time went on, however, and 'trouble' began to brew in the camp, their sympathies with the residents disqualified them as 'loyal' members of the staff.

Under such circumstances, the way an administrator gained familiarity with a resident was by collecting information about them. But what meant familiarity to the administrator spelt control to the resident.

With a limited staff of fewer than ten, and residents numbering over 250, only limited control was possible. The administration, however, had sole control over resources: possible job and accommodation opportunities. These opportunities were never advertised on the camp bulletin boards. The larger of the two boards displayed a notice in bold capital letters: HAVE YOU CONSIDERED EMIGRATING? And then gave a list of emigration opportunities to Sweden, Iran, Chile, Argentina, etc. The second board contained scores of short notices on internal camp affairs: meal times, committee meetings, etc.

Information about jobs and accommodation – information that a *resettlement board* should freely provide – was carefully guarded by the camp staff. Around it, an elaborate system of patronage developed. Access to this information was given as a reward to those who donated voluntary services. It was tacitly understood by all that voluntary services were not just confined to the physical work that would have to be done in any institution: washing, cleaning, keeping records, etc. Voluntary work also meant, to put it bluntly, informing on fellow residents: from reporting those who consumed more than their fair share of milk or took their food upstairs to their room, to noting down the names of those who spread 'dissatisfaction' about the camp. Not surprisingly, those who felt the most inadequate in the English environment, and the least able to carve out an existence for themselves, were the most apt to offer these services. Gradually, a most unhealthy environment developed.

On my second day at the camp, a friend, Ben and I were sitting in the room reading. Mr B, a voluntary messenger, came in and turned to my friend.

'You are wanted in the office.'

'Me? Why? I haven't done anything wrong. Did I do anything?' Written on his face, unmistakably, was the expression of fear. The camp administrator seemed omniscient. Or, as Ben put it more graphically: 'If I fart in this room, Mr Engel knows about it.'

For the first few days we were not really interested in the camp. What preoccupied our attention was the world outside the camp: Kensington High Street and Kensington Church Street. As time went on, however, it became impossible not to become aware of the camp, not just the people who lived in it, but the camp as an institution. The camp was run by a core of people hired by the Uganda Resettlement Board. The board had apparently decided that the top brass should be individuals familiar with Uganda, preferably with Uganda Asians. Given the historical relationship between Britain and Uganda, these people were inevitably colonial civil servants or soldiers. The administrator of the Kensington camp had previously been a CID officer in Uganda.

In the person of a colonial bureaucrat one found both the eternal quest of the bureaucrat for the perfectly ordered universe and the rather blunt conviction of a colonialist that there existed a natural hierarchy in the world, that some people were just born better than others. It was a view of the world that seemed to permit of only two kinds of people: friends or adversaries. In other words, you were guilty until proven innocent.

The staff was also all bureaucratic personnel, most of them highly trained in the administration of things. Together, they had successfully turned the camp into a total institution, like a prison or an insane asylum. With the distinction between private and public life obliterated, with all living subject to control and reduced to dependence, complete with an elaborate network of informers, the Kensington camp gradually became a nightmare in totally controlled living. There was no escaping the camp. On the face of it, life in the camp, with its surface calm and order, presented a sharp and favourable contrast to the open terror living in Uganda. But it was the Kensington camp, and not Amin's Uganda, which was my first experience in what it would be like to live in a totalitarian society.

8   THE CAMP II

ONE MORNING, splashed across the front pages of the newspapers, we read the headlines: 'Asians Too Comfortable in Camps' Too comfortable! It seemed a cruel mockery of people who had been uprooted and now disoriented by being thrown in the midst of a different society, an industrial society. Was Patel – the man who spent more and more hours in his bed with each passing day – too comfortable? But the situation of the residents was only one side of the coin. Besides this, there was also the structure of the camp, one that effectively discouraged the residents from themselves looking for ways to leave the camp and settle in the surrounding community.

Although Kensington was officially supposed to be a transit camp, and operated as such until November, in my two and a half months stay there, from November until January, it had in fact become a permanent camp. No more than one or two per cent of its residents had been transferred to another camp. In fact, in November, realising this fact, the staff itself started restructuring Kensington as a permanent camp. The point of the reorganisations was to create a long-term institution, based on the principle of self-help if possible. Innumerable committees were formed, each assigned to a specific task.

Everyone was supposed to 'donate' a certain amount of labour towards running the camp. Every other day, there would be a committee meeting, lasting anywhere from two to four hours. The meetings took place in the daytime, between 10am and 6pm, the working hours of the staff. What this meant was that, for those who were committee members, there was less and less time to go outside the camp. But the committee members were inevitably those who would otherwise spend their time looking for a job and accommodation outside the camp. The conviction of the staff that we would be long-term refugees was becoming a self-fulfilling prophecy. After two weeks as 'Chief Catering Officer,' I realised that I was truly becoming a 'refugee,' my existence increasingly remote from the world outside, the camp more my real world. I resigned, and was branded a troublemaker.

Of course, the staff of the camp did not actually set up those committees in order to prevent the active form seeking jobs. Perhaps they were just set up because the English love committees. From my point of view, however, the *intentions* of the staff mattered little; what counted were the *consequences* of their actions. An outsider, not having spent much time in the camps, could not be expected to know these structural factors. Perhaps somebody had asked a sample of Asians: 'Are you comfortable in the camps?' and received the reply, 'Yes,' or even 'Yes, we like the camps very much.' What this person may not have realised is that for a person brought up with an Indian tradition, it is merely polite to answer in the affirmative, especially if the question comes from one's host: the British or the board.

But the shortcomings of the camp were not just a result of misunderstanding. There were other and far more serious injustices meted out by the camp authorities. The most serious of these affected the detainees.

Among the residents of the camp there were a number who had been rendered stateless in Uganda, and were therefore officially detainees. Of 250 people in the camp, about 40 were classified as such. Being under detention meant that a person was allowed only an hour of freedom daily, an hour to leave the camp and go out into the streets. The camp administration ruled that if they volunteered to work in the camp, the detainees would be granted an extra hour of freedom.

The individual detainee was a person who had literally run from Uganda. Without documents, with minimal belongings, and no one to turn to for assistance, they felt trapped. The detainees were at the mercy of their host. In the immediate context of the camp, the administration represented the government. The primary question for a detainee was: will the British Government grant me permission to stay, or send me back to Uganda or elsewhere? Certainly a recommendation from the camp administrator would help. Every detainee was on their best behaviour.

The detainees, because of their circumstances, were both the most helpless and the most malleable people in the camp. They would do literally whatever they were asked to do. The camp administration took every possible advantage of the situation and devised a system whereby all dirty work, serving meals, washing kitchen utensils, arranging chairs, sweeping floors, acting as messengers for the staff, became the duty of the detainees. The single women detainees were to make tea three times a day for the staff. In return they were rewarded with an extra hour of freedom every day. The system, interestingly enough, was not just in the interest of the camp administration, but also in the interests of the holders of British passports in the camp who were given to understand that if the detainees did not do the work they would have to do it.

Needless to say, the detainees received no payment. All they received was the £2.10 social security which everyone else also received. This system continued smoothly for about six weeks. Then there were rumblings among the detainees. There were charges of forced labour and indications that they might stop work altogether. Precisely at that point, all but five of them were transferred to another camp, outside London, where they would not have easy access to press and public.

One of these remaining five was Mr B. He had worked as one of the catering staff. Now that I was resigning from my duties, would he care to work as the chief catering officer?

'Yes. I'd love to. But I have been told I must be an office messenger during working hours. I can't do both. Frankly, I'd prefer to work in the kitchen. It's less work and, also, it's more interesting.'

'We'll talk to the camp administrator then.'

At the next meeting of the catering committee, I raised the issue. The administrator, however, could not be convinced.

'Mr B has requested that he be allowed to stay in this camp, in London. He has agreed to work as a staff messenger, 9am to 5pm for five days a week. This is an agreement between him and me. If he wishes to be chief catering officer, he must find his own time for it.' Mr B remained a staff messenger.

At this point, three of us, all holding British passports, on the verge of starting jobs in London and therefore not susceptible to the wrath of the camp administration, decided to take the issue straight to the Uganda Resettlement Board headquarters. Through the help of Mr Praful Patel, the Asian member of the board, a meeting was arranged. Present were Mr Tim Critchley, Mr Patel, the camp administrator and the secretary of the board. I presented the case: the practice of the camp administration could only be described as forced labour. Admittedly, for the last two weeks these detainees had been paid (£5 a week for clerical workers and £2.50 for the staff messenger and women who made tea) but this payment was now discontinued; the detainees, should they choose to work, ought to be paid the market wage in London.

Astonishingly, the attitude of the board was that the detainees had been performing voluntary labour, that in fact they had asked to be allowed to work lest they become bored! We were told that it was an act of charity on the part of the board to keep the detainees occupied. As for payment, that had also been the board's generosity – 'nobody is paid for voluntary labour in London'. This generosity must now cease since the board had a commitment to the British taxpayer. It must economise. I could not help thinking of the early days of slavery when the institution was justified because it introduced the African to the *nobility of labour*; now, the satisfaction of labour, the release from boredom was the gift of the Uganda Resettlement Board to those detainees.

I must have looked noticeably bitter as the meeting came to an end. Mr Tom Critchley, the senior member present, turned to me: 'Look, there is no reason for a confrontation. You must compromise. That's the British way.'

Mr Praful Patel added, 'Yes, you are now British.' I hoped he was being cynical. If this was compromise, I wanted no part of it.

The board was not alone in seeing the refugees as a source of cheap labour. The idea had also occurred to others. At least twice a week, the camp would be visited by numerous people, Asian employers or Asian representatives of English employers, who usually ran dressmaking businesses. They came to find cheap female labour; on the surface, to offer assistance to unsuspecting and grateful women. Inevitably, they brought along an Asian employee who claimed to be extremely happy and maintained that with just a bit of overtime one could make a lot of money. Initially, we wondered why they were interested in hiring women and not also men. It soon became evident that they thought women would be more obedient, submissive and less likely to organise or publicise the entire operation. The work usually involved an apprenticeship of a few weeks when one would be paid, at most, a nominal wage. The payment, from the point of view of someone just arriving from Uganda, was quite generous. Given the cost of living in industrial England, however, it was pitifully low. Once all this became clear to us, the word passed around, and these prospective employers found an increasingly indifferent, sometimes even hostile, reception awaiting them.

9 A QUESTION OF IDENTITY

'GENERAL AMIN has nationalised British plantations in Uganda,' the word spread through the camp. At news time, the canteen was crowded. After explaining the substance of the general's latest decree and the nature of British interests affected, the BBC reporter proceeded to question the new African manager of a formerly British-owned tea plantation:

'The general maintains that Uganda doesn't need the British. If so, why weren't these plantations developed before the British arrived here? What were you doing then?'

The television interview ended. But the reporter's question was answered by one of the people in the canteen: 'They were on trees then.' It was the most extreme racial utterance I had heard from one of my compatriots. It was not simply the racial view of the world a person born and bred in colonial Uganda inherited. Amin's own brutal racism had intensified this racial consciousness. Put simply, the majority of Uganda Asians who came to Britain had become racialists through experience. The very first day I was in the camp, I remember Shivji, one of the people on my floor, saying, 'Africans are unfit to rule. Perhaps, the British should never have left Uganda.'

Sad, and yet angry, I retorted: 'Have you ever heard of what happened during the Indian partition, or what the Pakistanis did in Bangladesh, or the British in Ireland? Tell me, are Asians "fit to rule" in your terms?'

He shrugged his shoulders. I realised that an argument, no matter how persuasive in the abstract, would take us nowhere. But in the coming weeks it became clear that Shivji, among others, was in for another set of experiences, one that would shatter his view of the world.

In the next few weeks Shivji was one of the few people who started leaving the camp to see London and find himself a job. Gradually, he learned to travel by tube. At first, he noticed the inevitable writing on the wall: 'wogs out.' Once in a while he would realise that the tube was fairly crowded but the seat next to him conspicuously empty. After a few days, he learned that if you are coloured and are lost in a tube station it is better to approach a West Indian guard rather than his white counterpart. Every evening he would tell us about his experiences when we gathered after dinner. 'Some West Indians are really nice, aren't they?' he once remarked a little sheepishly.

That week, two Asian youths came to visit the camps. They had been born in Britain and wanted to know how the 'brothers' were doing. The conversation centred on the British: in Uganda and in Britain. Everybody was enjoying exchanging experiences. The common theme was the nastiness of the British. At this point, one of our visitors remarked:

'Yes, we blacks must unite and defend ourselves.'

'We blacks? What does he mean?' Patel turned to me.

'Yes, we. I mean nobody is really black. We are all different shades of brown. They call us coloured. We should call ourselves black and fight for Black Power.'

'Black Power?'

'Yes, look, we are from a group called the Black Liberation Front. All black people should unite in self-defence against the white power structure.'

Incredulous, Patel laughed: 'Are you crazy? I am not black. Nobody here is black. We are neither white nor black. We are brown.'

The visitor persisted: 'You don't understand...' The next half hour was quite bizarre. Like two lanes on a motorway, running parallel to one another, but with the traffic going in opposite directions, not meeting at any point.

During the evening get-together there were some remarks about our visitors from Shivji. 'I can believe that West Indians are nice people. But that we are all black! Phew!'

A few days later, Shivji received a letter from a friend who lived about 50 miles to the north.

'He is asking me to go visit him. He says he can find me a job and I can stay with him. I'll be back in two days. Patel, why don't you come with me? The board's not going to do anything for us, you know that. You will simply sit and rot.'

'I'll come. Why not? I have nothing else to do.' The day after, Shivji and Patel returned.

'Well, did you find a job?'

'Yes. But I don't know if I am going to take it. I think I want to live in a place where there are a number of our people.'

'What are you talking about?'

'Patel, you explain it.'

Patel sat down, legs crossed in a yoga position, as if ready to tell a long story:

'Well, you see, it was like this. Tuesday night, Shivji and I were walking around in this place. All by ourselves. I don't know what the English call the town. Anyways, we met four whites on the street. One of them turned to Shivji and said, "Hey blackie, what are you doing here? Why don't you go home?" Imagine, they called us *blackie*, not even *coloured*. We ignored them but they came up to us and this one said, "We'll teach you a lesson. We are going to beat you up." Four against the two of us. Some of these whites are tough. I started saying my prayers. Just then, as if God had answered, there came four West Indians. I think they had been following us and had listened to everything. One of them said to Shivji, "Don't worry, brother. We'll take care of them." But the whites had run away. And you know what this West Indian said? He didn't even ask our names, he simply said: "Look here, brother, it may have been different in Africa. But here, we are all brothers. For the white man, we are black. So forget this *coloured* shit."'

Shivji, who had been listening to Patel's account of the episode, added: 'Yes, Patel has said it. That's what happened. Maybe those liberation people have something to say. I don't care about the board. I am going to live in a Red Area.' (According to the lingo of the board, a Red Area is where there are 'too many coloureds'.)

Shivji had learned that the definition of race is social. In Uganda, we were Asians, and that meant being not-white and not-black. But here in England, we were simply not-white.

But there were others who differed from Shivji, who *did not* want to live in a Red Area. One weekend, Jagdish, my old friend from Kampala, came to visit us. He had gone to Bristol, determined to resettle himself. In the evening, I introduced him to the people on my floor. Patel made coffee and we sat and talked. At that point Jamal came in. He lived next door with his parents. His father had been affluent in Kampala, and had had an overseas bank account in Switzerland. They were in the camp 'for a few weeks while we look for a house'.

'Listen to the good news. We have found a house. Tomorrow we sign the papers.'

'Where is it?'

'Near Cockfosters. You probably haven't heard of the area. That's where a lot of rich English people live. There are no Asians there. It's a really good area.'

'What's good about there being no Asians there?'

'You don't understand. It's an upper class area. In an area with a lot of Asians, the property values go down. No English people want to live in such an area.'

When Jamal left, Jagdish remarked:

'Hm. A good area because there are no Asians there. What can one call it but self-hatred. Doesn't he realise he is an Asian? When he moves in, the whites will start leaving, and he'll be left there all by himself, with nothing but declining property values and other rich Asians moving in because "it is a good area".'

'Don't worry, Jagga. Jamal will learn.'

'I just wish everybody didn't have to *learn*. By the time we all learn we may be dead.' He paused, 'Have you heard of the Loughborough strike?' (This was a six-week strike of Asian hosiery workers towards the end of 1972. Its basic demand was 'equal treatment' with white workers in job allocation and promotion.)

'Of course I have. A lot of people here have been following it rather closely.'

'What do you think?'

'They are proud. Finally, some of our brothers are standing up to the white man.'

'You know, I went down there last week.' 'You did?'

He nodded, 'It's weird, man. The trade union is opposing our brothers and the management is with us. The last thing I expected was opposition from the English working class.'

'Well, you are wrong. Of course, theoretically, unions are supposed to be organisations of resistance, resistance to exploitation. But look at the practice. At Loughborough, at least, they seem to be playing the role of management – organised in defence of privilege, not in opposition to it.'

'Perhaps we should form Asian unions,' he paused and then laughed. 'That would be like back in Uganda, wouldn't it? The employers integrated, and the workers divided by race. The same old story: *divide and rule*.'

That Sunday we went to Hyde Park – to Speaker's Corner – where the blacks tell off the whites, and everybody departs amiably. To us, it

© Keystone/Hutton Archive/Getty

Smithfield meat porters march on the Home Office, bearing a petition calling for an end to all immigration into Britain, 25 August 1972

appeared a strange ritual of institutionalised hostility: to lead 'normal' lives for six days, and then on the morning of the seventh to let off steam.

We walked along the Bayswater Road, examining the long row of paintings that hung on the railings, finally making it to Speaker's Corner. There were groups of people all over the area. The size of the crowd around a speaker was the sole indication of their popularity. We walked to the fringes of the largest crowd. A Nigerian was speaking. We could hardly see him:

'This white man is asking me why I don't integrate. Why not? Come on, would you let me take your sister out?'

It seemed a well-practised evasion, but I couldn't help thinking the question had been put to the wrong person. The right person to answer that question is not the black but the white. The person to answer the question should be the person who, in fact, faces such a choice in real life. The poor do not have the choice of integrating with the rich, the rich do;

from the point of view of a person of colour, race and class coincide to a great degree in this country. The 'coloureds' do not have the choice of integrating with the whites, the whites do.

But I was not satisfied. Was I not still begging the question? If I had the choice, would I integrate? But that seemed too abstract a question, a half-hearted question. Integrate where? In England? When I am part of the unwanted minority? No, definitely not. Just one day out of the camp, a couple of nasty experiences, was enough to send us back to our 'kith and kin'. No wonder the camp became a fortress. No wonder people started thinking of settling in Balham, in Wembley, in Leicester and in Birmingham. And small wonder that once we started working we spent many weekends going to Southall. We were learning an elementary lesson, one that the poor and the weak learn all over the world: in a hostile environment, you stick together or, politically speaking, you organise.

'Wake up, Mahmood. It's cold, let's get out of here.' But I couldn't stop thinking. What bothered me was the hypocrisy around here. The papers for the last few days had been full of stories about a parliamentary revolt demanding a more liberal immigration policy for the 'old' Commonwealth, meaning the white Commonwealth. The government had responded by introducing a 'grandfather clause'. Essentially, this meant that if a resident of the white Commonwealth can document blood ties with England, that person can immigrate. But to the 400 or so Asian wives whose stateless husbands wait stranded in European camps, they say: 'Sorry, Britain is overpopulated.' What is an emphasis on blood ties but a racial emphasis? I remembered how they preached multiracialism to the newly independent East African countries, and how they counselled integration and racial tolerance to us in the camps. The victors always seem to forget that the vanquished have a longer historical memory. When they do realise it, they call it a complex.

When the question of the stateless husbands came up in the press, government ministers inevitably evaded the issue by bandying about well-practised phrases such as 'the characteristic generosity of the British people' or by referring to the record of 'British liberalism'. To us it seemed a bizarre experience to witness an attempt at national masturbation. In fact, to many of us who went through the 90 days in Uganda and came into English camps, the phrase 'British liberalism' seemed a contradiction in terms.

It was only later that I began to realise that this collection called the British people or the English people – the words *British* and *English* seemed interchangeable – was not exactly homogenous. As the weeks started rolling by, we began to realise that the camp authorities were doing precious little to resettle us. One of the volunteers suggested I call Westminster City Council, which had allocated subsidised housing for Uganda Asians. I called, only to be told that if I came through the Uganda Resettlement Board they would see me; if not I must wait in the queue, which I was told was quite long. The distinction was clear. For the board-sponsored Asians the accommodation could be immediate; the long queues, on the other hand, were for those English people who had probably been waiting for a while to get better housing. It dawned on me that the segment of the English people who were making the greatest sacrifice to accommodate us were the working people, not the affluent classes. The cost was being met by those who could least afford it.

I discussed these thoughts with Jagdish the next time I saw him. 'Imagine that! The redistribution is taking from the English poor to give to the penniless refugees. Do you wonder why the English working class views us with hostility?'

'Are you trying to explain away their racialism? Anyways, I can't be bothered. I am leaving this country.'

'Leaving this country? Where are you going?'

'To Sweden. I mean, I have applied to go there.' 'Why?' I asked.

'I am tired, man. My brother says I should get a factory job. Malik says I should go into business with him. I am sick of it all. In Kampala, I planned for the future. Now the future is here. What good has it done me to plan for it? I tell you, man, I am just packing my bags and leaving.'

'Yes, but why to Sweden?'

'There must be some difference between a country with no colonial history and another with a long colonial past,' he said with conviction. I couldn't disagree.

'When is your interview?' I inquired. 'Tomorrow.'

The next day when he came to see me, Jagdish was happy and gay.

'You made it?' I asked.

'Yes.'

'What did they ask you?'

'They asked me why I wanted to go to Sweden.' 'And what did you say?'

'I said it was the first European country to recognise North Vietnam.'

We laughed and walked towards the pub.

10   ON OUR OWN

I T WAS 20 December. I had spent seven weeks at the camp. There were others who had been there for as long as three months. In the first few weeks, we complacently accepted the administration's warning that Kensington was a transit camp and that we would soon be moved to another camp, where the process of resettlement would begin. But soon it became clear that the wait would be a long one.

With each passing day, one felt an air of permanence beginning to grow around the camp. A vegetable-like existence, where most of one's basic needs are catered to, gradually but successfully saps a person's sense of initiative. If the process continued for long, in time we would all become totally dependent on the good intentions of the Uganda Resettlement Board.

Not everybody was willing to accept these circumstances as the judgement of fate. Many, however, were even incapable of going out to look for a job and a place to live: they were either too old, or knew too little English, or both. I remember the feeling of despair on an elderly woman's face as she talked to me in my mother's room.

'Here son, sit here next to me. You know the ways of this place. Find me a job and I'll take care of myself. You ask your mother about me. I may look old, but these bones still have strength left in them. Listen, only eight years ago, in Kampala, after my youngest daughter had been married, I and my husband started living by ourselves. He was getting old and blind, and had stopped working. One day, I was left with nothing but 10 cents and some cooking oil in the house. Yes, only 10 cents and some cooking oil. You know what I did? I went and bought a half pound of potatoes. From these I made potato chips which I sold for 50 cents on the street. I bought more potatoes and sold the chips I made. That's how I started my business. My business was selling chips to children. In this way I managed to support myself and my husband. I never asked for any charity. If I had my way, I wouldn't spend another minute in this place. Just find me a job, son; cooking, cleaning, anything.'

© Chris Ware/Keystone/Getty

Members of the Uganda Resettlement Board pose in the Home Office, London
at their first formal meeting

Not all, however, were in such a desperate position. Gradually, one after another, people started moving out of the camp, following newspaper advertisements or contacting employment agencies. By 20 December, ten heads of families had found employment: as bank clerks, garage mechanics or department store attendants. All had started looking for accommodation. Four had succeeded. With their families, they were spending their last week or two in the camp, waiting for the day they would move out and begin a new life.

On the evening of 20 December, however, the camp authorities posted a notice in the two kitchens listing 50 names and instructing them to pack their belongings for they would be moved to another camp in the morning. It was 13 hours notice. We sought out the camp officials.

'Why do we have to move?'

'Because there may be European refugees coming from Uganda.'

'Why can't they be sent to other camps?'

'Because Kensington is the closest camp. And transportation is difficult over the Christmas period.'

'Why couldn't you have informed us earlier?'

The notice in the kitchen, however, said that the refugees were expected 'from India, the Middle East and other countries'. By late evening it became clear that, except for two, all those who had jobs, even those who had found accommodation (and were shortly to move out anyway) were listed among the 50. These people individually went and talked to the camp staff: could they please be replaced by others who had no job, who did not think they could get jobs in London, and who therefore wanted to leave the big city? But no, the administrative mind had been made up. Gradually, individuals formed into groups, and the groups coalesced into one meeting. A delegation was elected, consisting of four. We went up to the office and made the same request formally. The response, however, remained negative. Couldn't there just be a change in the specific individuals comprising the group, while the total number remained at 50?

THE GUARDIAN
Friday December 22 1972

Angry Asians refuse to move camp

By PETER COLE

UGANDA Asians at a London resettlement camp yesterday refused to be moved to another camp at Newbury, Berkshire after a day of protest meetings and talks with the camp administrator. They complained that they were given only 12 hours notice of the move and that they were being "treated like cattle".

Eventually they were issued with an ultimatum: they must leave today or face the consequences.

Text: © Guardian News & Media Ltd 1972

'No, the list is final.'

The machine had moved to a point of decision, but the officials were refusing to take a look at the merits of that decision. How could one explain to these super-bureaucrats that decision-making is not merely a question of accumulating facts? It is ultimately an act of choice.

As we sat in the room, the hour well after midnight, despair gradually gave way to collective resolve. It all seemed a repetition of Uganda, with one important exception: if we refused to leave Kensington, we would not be shot. It was clear that neither good arguments, nor goodwill meant anything to the camp authorities.

'What will happen if we refuse to leave?'

'I suppose they could call the police and force us to go.'

'But then we still won't be any worse off.'

'That's right. There is no way that we can be any worse off.'

'So we'll refuse to go.'

'But everybody must stick together.'

'Yes, everybody must pledge. Why don't we sign something?'

'A petition. These English like petitions. We'll put down all the reasons why we can't go, and then everybody will sign it.'

'But everybody should only mean those who really can't go.'

'OK, let's start. Mahmood, you know how to write. Why don't you write the petition. I will circulate it,' said Patel.

In a half hour the petition emerged. In another hour, it had been signed by six heads of families (representing 30 individuals) and ten single people.

We, the following residents of the Resettlement Camp at Kensington Student Centre respectfully decline to leave this camp for another this morning for the following reasons:

1. The overwhelming majority of us have been resident here for nearly two months. In this time, we have learned something of our environment. We have all either arranged for a job or are in the process of doing so. We are also attempting to arrange our accommodation. Going to another camp will mean spending another few months before we can once again get to this point. Our purpose is to leave this camp as soon as possible and not to move from camp to camp.

2. For our children, it will mean another interruption in their education.

3. Some of us have family members who are receiving medical treatment.

4. None of us have been given more than 13 hours' notice of our intended departure. We protest at being treated as objects or, at best, as cattle.

5. We hope that henceforth the camp administration will make some attempt to learn of our individual situations and problems before unilaterally adopting such drastic measures.

The next morning the bus came at the scheduled hour. We had all gathered in one room, refusing to talk to the camp administration except through the elected committee of four. In the early afternoon, the buses left – empty.

In the room, there was a feeling of euphoria, an air of celebration. For most people, this was the first time in their life they had ever gone against authority. And *white* authority at that. Peter Cole, a *Guardian* reporter who had been visiting the camp for the past few days, and had witnessed the event, was mobbed with questions:

'Will they call the police?'

'Oh, no, they can't.'

'You do think we did the right thing, don't you?'

The camp authorities, however, were infuriated by this act of defiance. To them, of course, it was added testimony that there were troublemakers among the camp residents. A conspiracy theory was the only alternative to looking at legitimate grievances. Meanwhile, another order had been issued: the original 50, and an additional 50 must leave the next morning. No list was put out. People were individually informed. Once again, there were protests. The committee of four and the camp staff met for over six hours that afternoon and evening.

'Why don't you let the people who have jobs stay behind?'

'But why can't they commute as most Londoners do? After all, it's only 60 miles from the Greenham Common Camp to London.'

How could I explain to this lady that it took the English people centuries of industrial capitalism before they could consider travelling 120 miles to and from work each day to be a normal experience?

'You realise how selfish you people are. You have enjoyed this place for quite a few weeks, some of you even for months. Now you are refusing to make way for some equally unfortunate people.'

'It is not a question of being selfish. We want to get out of these camps. If only you would give us at the most two weeks here we will find our own accommodation and get out. Many of us, in fact, will be out within a week.'

The same points were being made over and over again. It seemed as if we were involved in an elaborate dance – called a dialogue – that had to run the course of the evening before either side felt it could resume its original stance when the buses arrived the next morning.

But, suddenly, it seemed as if fresh orders had been transmitted from above. After a break lasting an hour, the meeting was resumed. The administrator, his upper lip a bit stiff, his tall but thin frame towering above us as he rose, spoke in carefully weighed words.

'Coaches are ordered for tomorrow. The Uganda Resettlement Board requires you to move tomorrow. Sir Charles Cunningham and the board in their wisdom have decided that you should leave these premises of the board for the other premises of the board. If you do not leave, there will be very serious consequences. This is a warning.'

It was almost a rehearsed performance. The voice of the administrator had echoed around the room, carrying the authority not just of his position but also of the resettlement board itself. I sat there wondering how matters could have gone so far. Surely, from the point of view of the board, this must appear to be a small point of disagreement. But one thing the hours of meeting had clarified was that it was not the content of our disagreement, but just that fact of it, that had infuriated the board.

We returned to our room, somewhat disturbed and angry. A staff member followed, asking permission to address the group informally. This informal talk, in fact, was a detailed recounting of statistics proving how the overwhelming majority of people who tried to settle by themselves had failed. The message was clear: it is foolishness to go it alone in the name of exercising initiative. Depend on the board and you shall receive all you want. This attempt at persuasion, however, failed. Once this fact was clear, there began a most extraordinary attempt at individual intimidation. A senior staff member visited the rooms of every dissenting person, talking at great length to all adult members of the family, particularly to wives and elderly parents, detailing all possible retaliatory measures the board could take against any family refusing to leave.

As the night wore on, it became clear that not everybody supported our decision to defy the board's orders. A minority believed that we ought to do as told even though it would be inconvenient. For what the board had given us, we ought to be grateful. From our point of view, their numbers indicated the extent of the board's success, for they were true refugees. Be grateful for anything, so they seemed to say. Particularly insistent was an elderly woman who had become a refugee during the Indo-Pakistani partition of 1946 and had then come to Uganda with her small children.

'If only you had been around then. In India there wasn't even a resettlement board. I tell you, you must do as they tell you to do.' But the rest of us were not willing to judge the board's performance by comparing it to the worst possible.

In the morning it became clear that the night work of the camp staff had begun to pay off. The people with families – those who had the most to gain by keeping their jobs, but the most to lose if the board just threw them out – agreed to leave on the morning bus. The young couples and single residents, responsible for nobody but themselves, decided to stay, determined to exercise their independence.

The press descended on us. The question was always the same. Aren't you being ungrateful, striking at the hand that has fed you? But what had been the nature of the board's generosity? Certainly, we had been fed, given winter clothing, a turkey on Christmas Day, even bus rides around London and shows for the children once in a while. But the generosity of the board had been of a particular kind, the sort of generosity that makes the giver feel good, while keeping the receiver dependent on further charity. Admittedly, the pleasure of an extravagant meal or a new coat is immense, but it is immediate and monetary. It does not change a person's long-term situation. The pleasure is short lived. Frustration with one's basic situation, which remains unchanged, follows.

One doesn't give a hungry man food, one gives him a job. The purpose of any worthwhile charity should be to undermine its own existence, not to ensure the continued dependence of its object. The generosity of the board, however, was seldom of such a nature.

Ironically, even when individuals found jobs and began to search for accommodation, the board invoked its obligation to that entity called the British taxpayer, charging these people for room and board in the camps. Furthermore, the bill was not just for the days after people had begun work, but for every day they and their family had spent in the camp. Such was the generosity of the board. The Uganda Resettlement Board can probably produce impressive figures to underline the success of its resettlement programme. Behind these statistics, however, lie not only a clever juggling of numbers but also a rather ugly reality.

According to the board, any person who ever registered in the camp and later left it, even if they stayed no longer than a day, was resettled by the board. Such a broad definition included large numbers of people who came from Uganda, rested for a few days in the camps and then left to join friends or relations. It also includes those who (once again in a sizable number) while staying in the camp found, of their own accord, jobs and accommodation in the surrounding area. Illustrative of its view of the refugees, the board simply takes them as passive objects, people without initiative, who could never resettle themselves, but are always resettled by the board.

An even uglier side of the picture is revealed when one realises the means by which the board resettled the remaining people. The most effective way the board had of resettling its charges was simply to transfer them to another camp. Transfers did not just take place when a camp closed down. There were people at Kensington for whom it was the fourth camp in two months. Faced with the prospect of being transferred to another part of the country, where it would take another few months before they became familiar with their surroundings and the opportunities these had to offer, a number of refugees simply packed up and left. The board had not resettled them as much as just got rid of them. As time went on, it became clear to us that the board's problem was not our problem. Their problem was us. If we would simply vanish into the air, whatever the means, they would be happy.

After experiences like this, it was easy to conclude that a part of the board's generosity – turkey at Christmas, televised magic shows for children, etc – was simply for press and public consumption, and that another part – feeding and clothing us and, after the initial exercise in resettlement, housing the rest of us – was simply a result of political necessity. Now that despite all the immigration acts and the enforced separation of families we were still here, we had to be dealt with somehow, lest we become like the Palestinian refugees.

The ordeal was not yet over. In the vocabulary of the camp administration, we had won and they had lost. The next week at breakfast one of the administrators sat at a table with a number of badges in front of him.

'Mr Mamdani, before you can have your breakfast, you must write your name on this badge and wear it on your shirt. And remember, you must wear it at all the times you are on the premises of the camp.'

'Why do we have to wear badges?'

'So that you can be identified and so that non-residents may not come and eat here.'

'Sir, the people who live and work around Kensington Church Street look like you, they do not look like us. I see no reason to wear this badge.'

'Then you will not be served breakfast.'

No breakfast it was. Outside I found a number of others who were also willing to defy the badge order. We met in my room. It was decided that I should go and see the camp administrator.

'Look, we are willing to compromise. We will carry cards for the sake of administrative efficiency, but will not wear badges.'

'Don't be petty, Mr Mamdani. What is the difference between a card and a badge? One is rectangular, the other is square. That is all.'

I knew the compromise would not be acceptable to the camp administrator, and in that I was right. I also knew that I was soon to leave the camp to write about it. I wanted nothing from the board, so I had no reason to fear it.

'I am sorry, but I will not wear a badge.'

It was once again clear that what infuriated the Uganda Resettlement Board was not the nature of the particular disagreement, but the fact of it. Disagreement to them was synonymous with insubordination and ingratitude.

The crux of the matter was that we had refused to act as refugees, as helpless, well-behaved children, totally devoid of initiative, indiscriminately grateful for anything that may come their way; in other words, dependence personified. In this scheme of things, we were the children and the board the shepherd. The board was the unselfish giver, while we were expected to stand to attention and respectfully appreciate the nobility of its sacrifice. It would all have happened according to the text, except that we were not refugees. Circumstances deprived us of our possessions, but not yet of our self-respect. For that last possession, our humanity, we were willing to fight. We would have to be made into refugees – but there would be no surrender.

A few days later, I left the camp. I came back to visit my remaining friends. Chakravarthy met me at the gate. His head was bandaged.

'What happened?'

'Haven't you heard? There was a big fight here yesterday evening. Four whites came down and they tried to beat up Singh, Patel and myself. They were skinheads.'

'Weren't the camp or centre staff around?'

'Yes, they were. They just stood and watched. What do you expect after all that has happened here? Come, I'll show you something,' he walked a few yards and pointed to a pool of dried out blood on the ground.

'Come on, everybody is out walking. We are all leaving this camp. I don't know where we are going, but we are going to resettle ourselves.'

We walked away from the camp. I looked back. The blood, dried and lifeless, lay on the tarred driveway, like a question mark.

ABOUT THE AUTHOR

© Chloe Aftel

Mahmood Mamdani is Herbert Lehman Professor of Government at Columbia University and was director and Professor at Makerere Institute of Social Research (2010-2022). He is the author, most recently, of *Neither Settler Nor Native: The Making and Unmaking of Permanent Minorities.* His other works include *Citizen and Subject: Contemporary Africa and the Legacy of Late Colonialism; Good Muslim, Bad Muslim: America, the Cold War and the Roots of Terror; Saviors and Survivors: Darfur, Politics and the War on Terror;* and *Define and Rule: Native as Political Identity.*

TITLES OF INTEREST FROM DARAJA PRESS

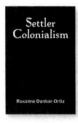

Settler Colonialism examines the genesis in the USA of the first full-fledged settler state in the world, which went beyond its predecessors in 1492. The text originates from Roxanne Dunbar-Ortiz (2021) "Not A Nation of Immigrants: Settler Colonialism, White Supremacy, and a History of Erasure and Exclusion."

ISBN-10: 1-990263-50-X • ISBN-13: 978-1-990263-50-7
$20 USD • $27 CAN • 61 pages

Insurrectionary Uprisings is a compendium of essays that explore what it will take to win a world based on love and justice. From historical writing, including Thoreau, Gandhi and Arendt, to essays that address the multiple crises we face in the 21st century, the volume brings together authors and thinkers from around the globe.

ISBN-10: 1-988832-99-3 • ISBN-13: 978-1-988832-99-9
$35 USD • $48 CAN • 490 pages

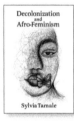

Sylvia Tamale's *Decolonization and Afro-Feminism* makes a compelling case for unlearning imperial power relations by shaking off the colonial filters through which we view the world. Tamale also proposes the African philosophy of Ubuntu to reinvigorate African notions of social justice. Winner of the 2022 FTGS Book Prize.

ISBN-10: 1-988832-49-7 • ISBN-13: 978-1-988832-49-4
$35 USD • $48 CAN • 420 pages

As the oldest (and arguably best-known) university in Uganda and the wider eastern and central Africa region, Makerere looms large in the history of higher education on the continent. This book explores the relationship between a public university of unique historical importance and the contestations over democratization that have taken place both within campus and beyond.

ISBN-10: 1-990263-16-X • ISBN-13: 978-1-990263-16-3
$27 USD • $37 CAN • 370 pages

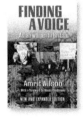

First published in 1978, *Finding a Voice* established a new discourse on South Asian women's lives and struggles in Britain. It explored family relationships, the violence of immigration policies, deeply colonial mental health services, militancy at work and also friendship and love. This new edition includes a preface by Meena Kandasamy, some historic photographs, and a remarkable new chapter titled 'In conversation with *Finding a Voice*: 40 years on'.

ISBN-10: 1-988832-01-2 • ISBN-13: 978-1-988832-01-2
$20 USD • $27 CAN • 288 pages

Order from **darajapress.com** or **zandgraphics.com**

Printed in the USA
CPSIA information can be obtained
at www.ICGtesting.com
LVHW020413071224
798552LV00003BA/507